D0728132

Especially for

....

Date

....

From

....

O Come Let Us Adore Him

Devotions Inspired by
"O Come, All Ye Faithful"

PAMELA L. McQUADE

BARBOUR BOOKS
An Imprint of Barbour Publishing, Inc.

INTRODUCTION

O come, all ye faithful
Joyful and triumphant,
O come ye, O come ye to Bethlehem!
Come and behold Him,
Born the King of angels;
O come, let us adore Him,
O come, let us adore Him,
O come, let us adore Him,
Christ the Lord.

Experience anew the wonder of the Christ Child's birth with this generous offering of 180 devotional readings, paired with relevant scripture selections, inspired by the beloved Christmas hymn "O Come, All Ye Faithful." Each reading shares an uplifting message that will touch your heart this Christmas.

O Come, All Ye Faithful

COME

"Come to me, all of you who are weary and
over-burdened, and I will give you rest!
Put on my yoke and learn from me.
For I am gentle and humble in heart and
you will find rest for your souls.
For my yoke is easy and my burden is light."

MATTHEW 11:28–30 PHILLIPS

God isn't "way out there," uninterested in our lives. Though the world may tell us God is some distant being who doesn't care about humanity, the Bible says nothing could be further from the truth. Our loving Lord wants us to know Him in intimate detail, so He sent us His Son and called us to come.

God knows how weary sin makes a human life, so He sent Jesus to lift the burden and bring us back to Him. Though our yoke of sin is heavy, God lifts it from our shoulders. His burden is light because we share it with the Savior.

Answer His call, and He will lighten your load.

ETERNAL-LIFE JOYS

You study the Scriptures diligently because
you think that in them you have eternal life.
These are the very Scriptures that testify about
me, yet you refuse to come to me to have life.

JOHN 5:39–40 NIV

As we celebrate Christmas, that special joy of knowing that the Savior came to give us entrance into eternity fills our hearts.

But that's not the universal response to the holiday, because many who outwardly celebrate Christmas have missed out on having Jesus in their hearts. They're going through the motions, perhaps because they don't know what else to do. Though they have heard the story, they've never come to the One who tells it, or they simply do not understand the need to do so.

In this holy season, Jesus reaches out to many confused doubters through those who have already come to Him. His people are the arms that draw them into His love.

THE WHOLE PACKAGE

"And anyone who believes in God's Son has eternal life.
Anyone who doesn't obey the Son will never
experience eternal life but remains
under God's angry judgment."

JOHN 3:36 NLT

*I*nto that tiny baby born in a stable God packed His whole salvation package. By being God's Son, rather than an ordinary child, Jesus forever redefined faith. After the sacrifice He made on the cross, only belief in Him brought eternal life to humanity.

That can be an uncomfortable truth for many people who would rather have their religion in another, less threatening package. They don't want God to demand too much of them or to set them apart from others. But along with that unthreatening babe comes all of Jesus' ministry and His death and resurrection. You can't take the sweet baby without also taking the bitter cross.

Still, this truth is a wonderful thing. For without the whole package—bitter and sweet—we'd never know the full meaning of God's merciful love.

GIVING ALL

For thou shalt worship no other god: for the LORD,
whose name is Jealous, is a jealous God.

EXODUS 34:14 KJV

When God calls us to faithfulness, He expects it to be complete. He makes no allowances for us to slip into heresy or syncretism. And we cannot decide to replace His love with materialism or the affections of any human, as wonderful as that person may be.

When Jesus came to save us, He gave everything— He became a baby, limiting Himself to our physical and emotional dimensions. He lived in poverty and placed Himself at risk from His enemies.

As we recognize the greatness of His sacrifice, perhaps we can begin to understand why the Father asks so much of us, too. For Him to do any less would be to disparage His Son's sacrifice, to denigrate the costly sacrifice that restored the God-to-human connection broken in Eden.

Knowing how much He gave, can we offer less than all our worship and love?

SPECIAL SON

But when the fullness of the time had come,
God sent forth His Son, born of a woman,
born under the law, to redeem those who
were under the law, that we might
receive the adoption as sons.

GALATIANS 4:4–5 NKJV

Jesus' birth was all about timing. Really, He could have come almost any day, because people always needed the salvation. But God chose a particularly dark time in the history of Israel. The nation had been conquered by the powerful and pagan Roman Empire. Sin flourished, and faithful Jews easily could have given up. Into this environment, God sent His Son to fulfill the promise in Genesis 3:15.

Into that dark time came a bright Son, born of a seemingly ordinary woman, in the poorest of circumstances. But God didn't need a fancy place for His Son to be born. It was His Son who was special, the bright and shining star of salvation.

It's the same today, in our dark times.

LIFELONG FAITH

And now, just as you accepted Christ Jesus
as your Lord, you must continue to follow him.
Let your roots grow down into him, and let
your lives be built on him. Then your faith
will grow strong in the truth you were taught,
and you will overflow with thankfulness.

COLOSSIANS 2:6–7 NLT

Faith in Jesus is not a one-shot thing. You don't walk down an aisle or say a prayer and end your spiritual life. Just as the child in the manger was a beginning, so is coming to faith in Christ.

Daily we need to sink our spiritual roots into Him and grow in faith that lasts for a lifetime, through good days and purely miserable ones. As we rejoice in the good days and struggle to remain faithful in miserable ones, we develop into sturdy trees grounded in His truth.

Then, as Christ shows through our lives, that truth may affect others, shading them with encouragement in hard times, and we will all give thanks.

TURF WARS?

When Herod the king had heard these things,
he was troubled, and all Jerusalem with him.

MATTHEW 2:3 KJV

When Herod squirmed at the idea that another king contended for his throne, Jerusalem writhed. This insecure ruler had a terrible history of violence, and the city didn't want him taking his aggravation out on them. Right under his thumb, they could hardly escape disaster.

Throughout His life, this child the wise men sought would threaten not only the nation's ruler, but Israel's spiritual leaders, too. Centuries earlier the prophets had disturbed Israel's false peace with messages from God, and its spiritual leaders had resisted. Thirty years later, Israel's leaders would rebel against Jesus' advent onto their turf as He began His ministry.

If we feel our spiritual turf has been threatened, let's remember these men. Though they knew the scriptures, fear of losing their power made them miss out on the greatest thing God would do in their lifetimes. If we feel threatened, will we miss the best He has for our lives?

LOVE

This is my commandment,
That ye love one another,
as I have loved you.

JOHN 15:12 KJV

The holidays are a time for family, and that can be a wonderful thing if your family consists of people you love to be with. But as families grow, sometimes you end up with that cousin by marriage you'd really rather not spend a lot of time with. Or if there's a divorce in the family, you can end up feeling very uncomfortable.

Human relationships can be very challenging, and God knows it. So He calls us to a universal response—loving one another in Him.

Maybe you won't want to invite that cousin to your home every week for Sunday dinner. And you won't feel warm fuzzies about the divorce. But you can ask God to help you treat those people kindly, for the sake of the family members for whom you do feel affection.

For a short time, you can show others love. And in the end, you may find they're not so bad.

God's amazing like that.

GOOD, PLEASING, AND PERFECT

Don't copy the behavior and customs of this world,
but let God transform you into a new person by changing
the way you think. Then you will learn to know God's
will for you, which is good and pleasing and perfect.

ROMANS 12:2 NLT

When God comes into our lives, it's as if we had a massive washing day. He cleanses us from top to bottom, and we feel as clean as a newly squeegeed glass window. But we also have a part in the creation of this new, clean person; we have to allow God to transform our lives, and we must cooperate with Him.

On Christmas Day, God gave the world a new start. Some people recognized it and made Him the power in their lives. Others simply ignored the birth of the new King. Which we do is our choice, but only one brings us into line with God's will, which is good, pleasing, and perfect for our lives.

THE BEST WAY

"Turn to me and be saved,
all you ends of the earth;
for I am God, and there is no other."

ISAIAH 45:22 NIV

For many people, Christmas is a wonderful time of faith. But what of those who have fallen for Santa-ianity instead of Christianity? Their experience of Christmas is quite different from the faithful believer's.

God does not call us to worship at the altar of St. Nick. The real saint of that name has little to do with the fat, red-suited fellow. Saint Nicholas gave to people in real need instead of encouraging people to overspend on others who are already prosperous. And in Nicholas's day, the nation's economy didn't depend on year-end spending for stores to get into the black financially.

At Christmastime God does not call on us to do anything but worship Him. Whether this is a personally profitable year or a lean one, we can still do that. Then we will have celebrated Christmas in the best way—the one that honors Jesus.

A PRIVATE CHOICE

And all who heard it were amazed at
what the shepherds said to them.

LUKE 2:18 NIV

The shepherds shared the message given to them by the angels, just as they were meant to. And those with whom they shared the story were amazed.

We share the same message the shepherds received. Some people, often those who have been seeking God, will be amazed and come to faith. Some will want to learn more. Others reject the story, calling it unbelievable.

We cannot make anyone else's decisions. Each has to make a private choice concerning faith. We simply place the choice before others in such a way that they can understand its importance and be encouraged to make a good decision. No manipulating on our part brings a soul to God. In prayer and trust in God lie our hopes. But we hope in the Lord who sent angels to peasants who reached their nation with the Good News.

Our hope in the Lord is never in vain.

GRANITE HEARTS

*Now faith is the substance of things hoped
for, the evidence of things not seen.*

HEBREWS 11:1 KJV

No wonder unbelievers sometimes think we're crazy. We believe in things we can't see, touch, or prove by worldly means. God's message makes no sense to someone who has never experienced the Savior, because we Christians see with our hearts, not our eyes.

God brings His evidence into our lives, and we believe, like the shepherds who followed angels' directions. But those who have never heard the "voices of angels" have nothing to show them the way.

We can speak all the words in the world, and some will never believe. Our speech cannot convince them. Should we somehow argue them into a corner, they would still resist, because only when God's Spirit applies the truths to unbelievers' hearts do they open wide to Him.

Know some people who sturdily resist the faith? Faithful prayer is the best recourse. Truly, only God can crack those granite hearts.

WONDERFUL
TESTIMONY

*Many, LORD my God, are the wonders you
have done, the things you planned for us.
None can compare with you; were I to speak
and tell of your deeds, they would
be too many to declare.*

PSALM 40:5 NIV

At Christmastime, when we see the lengths God
went to in order to bring us to Himself, it's easy
to sing of His wonders. It's not hard to delight in God
when we see examples directly before us. But what
about the rest of the year, when celebrations don't
keep our minds on those wonders? Will we still remember the good things God gives His people?

We don't need to shop for presents or put up
trees yearlong. But we can recount our own salvation
experience and see how He has worked in the lives of
others by reading scripture and biographies of those
fellow faithful ones.

The testimony of God's wonders is always there,
among the faithful.

BE FAITHFUL

*"But be sure to fear the LORD and
serve him faithfully with all your heart;
consider what great things he has done for you."*

1 SAMUEL 12:24 NIV

The people of Israel had a long relationship with God. They had heard of how He rewarded their forefathers' faith. As children, their bedtime stories told of the way God parted the Red Sea for their people. Then He had promised them a land and helped them conquer the nations in it.

Whether we are the first people in our families to know God or come from a long line of believers, we too have a history with God. For us, He sent His Son to a stable in Bethlehem and onto a cross in Jerusalem. Through our lives as Christians, He has shown Himself faithful to us, parting our Red Seas and making a way into a new life.

For this, He only asks us to remember and be faithful.

Is that too hard to do?

FOCUS ON THE GIFT

Do not love this world nor the things it offers you,
for when you love the world, you do not have the love
of the Father in you. For the world offers only a craving
for physical pleasure, a craving for everything we see,
and pride in our achievements and possessions.
These are not from the Father, but are from this world.

1 JOHN 2:15–16 NLT

If ever there was a time of year when cravings loom large, it's at Christmas. Temptations constantly grab at us, whether we are shopping for gifts or standing in line at a buffet.

Step back from the worldly Christmas that focuses on Santa, gifts, and pleasures of this world, and remember what the holiday is all about: a baby in a manger, not a competition to buy the best gift; God's salvation, not buffets full of food.

Focus on Jesus, God's gift to you, and His love returns to your heart. Suddenly temptation loosens its grasp.

CHRISTMAS GIFTS

And this world is fading away,
along with everything that people crave.
But anyone who does what pleases
God will live forever.

1 JOHN 2:17 NLT

What did you get for Christmas last year? Can you even remember? What did your children get? Can they tell you?

Chances are pretty good that the things you or your family just had to have are no more than a faint memory. They may even be broken and long since put in the trash or stuffed at the back of a closet.

But if you received a special spiritual gift, like a sermon that convicted you or challenged you to grow, you may still have its benefit in your life. Even if you don't remember all its details, it changed you.

The world may fade away, but God's gifts last. They may not come wrapped in pretty packages, but they'll last in your life forever.

A FAITHFUL RHYTHM

Be joyful in hope, patient in affliction,
faithful in prayer.

ROMANS 12:12 NIV

What does it mean to be a faithful Christian? This verse gives us a good picture of how we can glorify God daily. No matter what goes on in our lives, it describes how we should respond.

The Christian life has many facets. In good times, we happily hope in God, our Savior and help, but trials also come our way and test our patience, so through the hard parts of life we consistently stand firm in Him. And no matter what life brings us, we remain faithful in prayer, our pipeline to God.

A faithful life can be either very exciting or extremely ordinary. But beneath it all should be this rhythm of hope, patience, and faith, underlying our lives as we move from one event to another.

Have you found that faithful rhythm in your life?

REJOICE OR MOURN

Rejoice with those who rejoice;
mourn with those who mourn.

ROMANS 12:15 NIV

Christmas is a season of high—and low—emotions. If life is going well, and a family is happy and has much to be thankful for, joy may easily be in order. But for others who have reason to sorrow, Christmas may be the most difficult time of the year.

Scripture tells us to share the joy or sorrow of our fellow Christians. With young and happy families, we easily share the delights of the season. But with those who grieve, we also have something to share—the gentle love of the One who is always there, even when sadness floods our lives.

Jolly holidays are pleasant, but they are not the only side of Christmas. If that were so, we'd only have to rejoice with the joyful. But Jesus, the tenderhearted Savior, stands by hurting hearts in a happy season. And we should, too.

HOLIDAY WITNESS

And now these three remain: faith, hope and love.
But the greatest of these is love.

1 CORINTHIANS 13:13 NIV

In all the messages that clang loudly about us at Christmastime as the TV broadcasts annoying ads and our inboxes are overloaded with even more calls to buy, buy, buy, the most powerful message gently reaches out to our hearts. God announces above the din of mall Christmas music that love is what we're really seeking.

All the gifts in the world can't fill the God-sized space in our hearts. Only Jesus fits there, and though He's what the season is all about, it's easy for people to miss that truth in the holiday white noise that drowns out Christmas's real point.

As we're in contact with others during this season, let's remember to treat them with love. In the shopping malls or church, if we keep love in mind and treat others as those whom Jesus loves, our actions will reflect the gentle message of the real meaning of Christmas.

FAITHFUL HEARTS

To the faithful you show yourself faithful;
to those with integrity you show integrity.

PSALM 18:25 NLT

What's the point of being faithful and having integrity in a world where those qualities seem unimportant? we may ask ourselves during the holidays, when we see others being less than perfectly honest and feel taken advantage of because we won't act that way. We may even wonder what benefit there is to having faith.

But the question we need to ask isn't really "What can we get away with?" It's "How does God call us to live?" Being taken advantage of during the holidays by less-than-honest people is not appealing, but another's dishonesty still isn't reason for us to lose our spiritual bearings.

God promises that when we are faithful to Him, He will be faithful to us. When we show integrity, so will He. So let's keep our hearts faithful because it's the right thing to do, something God can bless us for.

BARGAIN BASEMENT?

And without faith it is impossible to please God,
because anyone who comes to him must believe that he
exists and that he rewards those who earnestly seek him.

HEBREWS 11:6 NIV

This verse may seem like a no-brainer. Of course you need to believe in God and His rewards.

But how many people claim to be Christians yet barely show a sign of faith?

Our Lord isn't looking for people who want to go to church on Easter and Christmas, then forget Him the rest of the year. Living as a Christian means commitment; the Christian life demands earnest seeking and faith that doesn't end when hardship comes.

God isn't more foolish than the humans He created. He knows real faith when He sees it and rewards it with eternity. So please yourself or please God, but never expect to earn a cheaper heaven. There's no bargain basement in eternity.

REAL CHRISTMAS

Jesus said, "Let the little children come to me, and do not hinder them, for the kingdom of heaven belongs to such as these."

MATTHEW 19:14 NIV

Children had a special place in Jesus' heart, so when people say, "Christmas is for children," in part they are right. Christmas is for everyone who comes to Jesus with an open heart.

But most people who say that aren't speaking from a spiritual point of view. True, children do enjoy Santa and all the presents. But that isn't the full meaning of Christmas, and a curious child looks beyond the gift wrap to find it.

Even for children, Christmas is not merely about a man in a red suit and gifts. Don't underestimate a child's spiritual perception—this holiday need not simply be Santa focused. The children in your life may be curious about the other side of Christmas, even if they don't ask.

So be ready to share the real Christmas—the one with Jesus in it.

MISSION COMPLETED

"You will conceive and give birth to a son,
and you are to call him Jesus. He will be great
and will be called the Son of the Most High.
The Lord God will give him the
throne of his father David."

LUKE 1:31–32 NIV

For any woman, this would have been amazing news, but for a humble young peasant in a small, quite secular town, news that she would bear the long-awaited Messiah, the Most High's Son who would rule Israel, must have been even more stunning.

God bypassed women with more education and more worldly skills for Mary. We know nothing of her background or her credentials for the job, but her praise in Luke 1:46–55 tells us she had profound faith and spiritual depth.

When God calls us to do His will and we don't feel capable, will excuses die on our lips, as they did on Mary's? She completed her mission faithfully—and we can complete ours, if God is with us.

COSTLY GIFTS

When you ask, you do not receive, because
you ask with wrong motives, that you may
spend what you get on your pleasures.

JAMES 4:3 NIV

Just as we won't buy a Christmas gift that would harm our child, God won't give us, His children, anything that would harm us.

When our motives are less than pure and more pleasure seeking, God knows that giving us what we desire will be as much a danger to us as a two-wheeled bike would be to a three-year-old. We won't find what we most desire under the tree.

Though it's hard to wait to see a dream come true, perhaps we need to ask ourselves why we want this great "Christmas present." Will we have to give up something precious for that house we earnestly desire? Spending time with our families, because we have to work longer hours to afford it? Attending our children's soccer games, because we have more yard work to do?

Sometimes this world's gifts come with a price. Should we pay it?

SANTA OR SAVIOR?

Some have departed from these and have turned to meaningless talk. They want to be teachers of the law, but they do not know what they are talking about or what they so confidently affirm.

1 TIMOTHY 1:6–7 NIV

There's a fair amount of "meaningless talk" surrounding Christmas. Stories and legends that have nothing to do with the real meaning of the holiday confuse those who have never heard the Gospel message, and doubtless many who have little connection with the church believe that Santa is what the holiday is all about.

Let's be sure our congregations' children have a clear idea that knowing Santa and knowing Jesus are not the same thing. Do our church programs make it clear who the Savior is, or are they so filled with Christmas trees, ornaments, and gifts that a child could miss out on the real gift, Jesus? Would a visitor clearly understand our Advent message? Will children whose only contact with Jesus is through our church come to love Santa or the Savior?

OPEN HANDS

*You have taught children and infants to tell of your
strength, silencing your enemies and all who oppose you.*

PSALM 8:2 NLT

*E*ven children can give testimony to God, especially
at this season. They may not be able to argue theology, but our young ones understand the basic things in
life, and Jesus is one of them. Simple faith reaches into
places no debate can touch.

We all come to God with childlike faith, reaching
out in hope to the Father. When we come to God, all
the education and arguments in the world are fruitless.
Only empty hands can reach out to the Savior. And
God's gift is easily placed in them.

This Christmas, open your hands to the simple but
profound message of the Lord, and your life will be
filled.

LOVED BEST

In every nation he accepts those who fear him and do what is right. This is the message of Good News for the people of Israel—that there is peace with God through Jesus Christ, who is Lord of all.

ACTS 10:35–36 NLT

Christmas is celebrated around the world, wherever people believe in Jesus. As the largest religion in the world, Christianity touches 2.18 billion people, according to the Pew Research Center, which also says that in the last century, "Christianity has grown enormously in sub-Saharan Africa and the Asia-Pacific region. . . . Christianity today—unlike a century ago—is truly a global faith."

No matter what nation believers live in, God accepts them. He won't favor one nationality over another, just as loving parents won't favor one child over another in the family.

At this season of peace, every child of God is loved best, because God made each of us and loves us for who we were meant to be. Let's treasure that news and share it with the world.

Joyful and Triumphant
CALLED TO JOY

You make known to me the path of life;
you will fill me with joy in your presence,
with eternal pleasures at your right hand.

PSALM 16:11 NIV

*B*efore you knew Him, joy wasn't the first thing you connected with Jesus. Perhaps you feared Him or thought He was a killjoy. That's an unbeliever's view of our Lord, because those who don't know Him have never experienced the joy of being forgiven and knowing the Lord of the universe.

Salvation is such a wonderful gift that believers' hearts delight in it. Freedom from sin, a relationship of the deepest love anyone can experience, and an eternity shared with the Beloved—who wouldn't delight in that?

When God calls us to joy, He isn't limiting it to one special season—though celebrating Christmas certainly contains its own special delight. For the Christian, joy is a way of life, because we know our Lord every day of the year.

Let's make the most of that joy for all 365 days.

EARLY RAIN

Be glad, O sons of Zion. Be happy in the Lord
your God. For He has given the early rain to
help you. He has poured down much rain for
you, both fall and spring rains, as before.

JOEL 2:23 NLV

If you had to rephrase this verse in city-slicker terms, it might read: "Be happy, believers, be happy in your God. For He has provided for you."

God cares for us in many physical ways, though we may not be farmers who wait for rain. As we look back on the year that has led up to Christmas, are we mindful of the ways God has brought us happiness as He has provided for us? Have we gotten a new job? Found that we had just enough money to pay our bills? Seen things work out that we never expected would? Then let's be happy in the Lord our God. After all, He provided it all.

CHRISTMAS DELIGHT

Delight thyself also in the LORD: and he shall give thee the desires of thine heart.

PSALM 37:4 KJV

Christmas is a time of many delights: the giving and receiving of gifts, holiday celebrations, church services that are filled with joy. It's easy to be on a spiritual high.

Though some unbelievers portray Christianity as a doom-and-gloom religion, nothing could be further from the truth. God has given His people the greatest gift: His Son. And though doom-and-gloomers may not understand, faith is something to celebrate. All the gifts and joys of the season pale compared to the real delight believers find in drawing near to Jesus.

As we gather together to celebrate and focus on Jesus, joy floods our souls. As we delight in Him, not the earthly trappings of Christmas, our hearts receive their greatest desire—a closer relationship with Him.

No one loves us as deeply and thoroughly as Jesus.

GOD-GIVEN VICTORIES

*Therefore, brothers and sisters, in all our
distress and persecution we were encouraged
about you because of your faith.*

1 Thessalonians 3:7 NIV

This is a time of year when you're likely to hear stories of Christians who have stood firm in their faith and were blessed for it. When we hear of faith in the face of challenges, our hearts are encouraged, whether it's a family member who tells her story or a complete stranger. It doesn't take a Christian rock star or famous pastor to make a story warm our hearts.

That's the way it is in the faith, the way God designed it. As brothers and sisters, we should share our God-given victories, not to raise our own stars in the Christian firmament, but to encourage those who experience a similar trouble. Hearing of the success the Thessalonians experienced, Paul and his co-laborers were lifted up. So others will feel, too, when we share how God has blessed our lives.

REJOICE!

Always be full of joy in the Lord. I say it again—rejoice!

PHILIPPIANS 4:4 NLT

*R*ejoice! That's the message Paul gave the Philippians when he wrote them about how they should live as Christians. Though Paul penned his epistle from prison and the Philippians were persecuted (1:12–30), the apostle prescribes a joyful attitude because they have received the salvation that secures their eternal home. With no concerns about their future destination, they have the freedom to rejoice.

How much more can we have joy, without having to worry every day if our lives will be required of us? And in a season when our thoughts are constantly on Advent, we have many good things to remind us of the future God has prepared for us.

So even when we're stressed out about Christmas shopping, family gatherings, or Christmas traffic, let's remember to rejoice. As Christians, it is our privilege and our delight.

A NEW SONG

He put a new song in my mouth, a hymn of
praise to our God. Many will see and fear
the LORD and put their trust in him.

PSALM 40:3 NIV

The praise of the angels at Jesus' birth extends to praise on earth as our hearts are filled with joy at the understanding of all He saved us from. As we sing of Jesus' birth, our voices easily sound out in joy. But are holidays the only times we sing God's praises?

When David wrote this verse, he had patiently waited for help from God during a dire situation. God came through for him, and it was as if David's salvation was new all over again. So he praised God aloud, hoping others would hear his joy and come to know Him.

Let's not be slow to praise God when He has been faithful to us and saved us from a horrible situation. We can sing that new song all year.

JOY DELAYED

Why art thou cast down, O my soul?
and why art thou disquieted in me?
hope thou in God: for I shall yet praise him
for the help of his countenance.

PSALM 42:5 KJV

Maybe Christmas isn't a time of joy for you this year. Perhaps you've recently lost a loved one or a family situation makes holiday gatherings difficult. Whatever your sorrow, take heart!

God has not deserted you. Though depression fills your soul today, His help will not fail. If sorrow fills your path now, it can soon turn to joy. God's help lies somewhere in the future, and if you trust in Him, it is certain to find you.

Don't let the pressures of one day of the year get you down. Trust in the Savior who brings salvation to your whole life, and the joy that's delayed will return again.

A SACRIFICE OF PRAISE

I will sacrifice a voluntary offering
to you; I will praise your name,
O LORD, for it is good.

PSALM 54:6 NLT

Sometimes praising God is a sacrifice when our hearts don't quite feel up to it. Yet we know we should praise Him, for we have a wonderful history of good things He's done in the past.

Christmas is a time of high expectations. Everyone wants us to be joyous and happy. But life doesn't always go along with the plan. Troubles come to us at holidays as well as every other day of the year.

That's why we need to remember who God is and what He has done for us. We may not be perky about our situation, but we can be thankful for the ways in which God has been faithful, and that gives us reason to offer Him a holiday sacrifice of praise.

CAUSE TO REJOICE

"The LORD is my strength and song, and
He has become my salvation; He is my God,
and I will praise Him; my father's
God, and I will exalt Him."

EXODUS 15:2 NKJV

Once they were safe on the far side of the Red Sea, safe from the Egyptian soldiers, Moses and his people stopped and became one huge choir, singing this hymn of praise. Just as we praise God at Christmas for sending us Jesus, our Savior, the Israelites recognized that God had saved them from physical and spiritual bondage in Egypt.

Salvation of both body and soul and the worship that follows is one of the Bible's recurring themes. Remember, for example, Noah and the ark, the conquest of the Promised Land, and the return of Judah to Israel after exile in Babylon.

Perhaps our causes for rejoicing are not as big as the Red Sea crossing, but the Lord still enjoys hearing our joyful song.

IT'S YOUR CHOICE

This is the day which the LORD hath made;
we will rejoice and be glad in it.

PSALM 118:24 KJV

Are you planning on having a joy-filled day? Or does the idea of all that rejoicing just fall flat?

If rejoicing doesn't appeal to you, life's experiences may have gotten in the way of God's plans. God has given you this day for joy. In it you can bring happiness to others or make them miserable, too. You can share His love or turn everyone else's smiles into frowns just like yours.

The psalmist assumes we'll make the best of each God-given day, taking joy in our Savior and letting that joy fill our lives and the lives of others as our spirits reflect His. But it's up to us. We can let the negativity of life take over our hearts, or we can let our hearts sing for Him.

Which will you be doing today?

SHARE THE JOY

The commandments of the LORD are right,
bringing joy to the heart. The commands of the
LORD are clear, giving insight for living.

PSALM 19:8 NLT

When we pick up our Bibles, are we ready for joy? If not, maybe we should look for it. Because reading the Word should bring joy as we learn of the blessings God has in store for us. And even when He turns our lives around, we can rejoice that we've started down a better path.

Maybe we won't be rocking the rafters with praise every day, but a gentle course of joy can undergird our spiritual lives. Knowing the love of the Lord and having a life direction bring peace to our hearts and spirits.

Every morning, as we open the Word anew, we can look for something wonderful, and the drudgery of Bible reading disappears. God wants us to share the joy of the words He has written just for us.

HEIGHTS OF BLESSING

For He has regarded the lowly state of His maidservant; for behold, henceforth all generations will call me blessed.

Luke 1:48 nkjv

Mary didn't worry about the role God gave her when He chose her to bear His Son. Though she keenly felt her own humble stature, she was also aware of the blessing God had graced her with. This humble young woman had just the right stuff to raise His Son: she was ready for God to use her.

When God gives Christians something to do, if we have proud attitudes, we are quite likely to fail. We can never do His work in our own power. But when we recognize our own weakness, seek His help, and follow His commands, we cannot fail.

The blessing is not our own ability, but the work of His Spirit in our lives. He alone raises the humble to the heights of blessing, a place we can never reach on our own.

REGULAR DIET

But his delight is in the law of the LORD;
and in his law doth he meditate day and night.

PSALM 1:2 KJV

*D*o we take joy in God's Word, or is it simply a duty to read it? Are we ready to search out what it says, or do we see it as a restriction on our lives?

How we view His Word tells a lot about the way we feel about God. On days when God seems so close we could touch Him, we feel the joy of His Gospel. On days when we struggle, we may grasp His Word for solutions and be thankful for what we find there. But when despair seems too close for comfort, our joy slips away, and God seems distant.

No matter how we feel, we need to make scripture reading a regular diet. In each of these cases it may work differently, but it is always important. Whether we feel the joy or need it, the Word draws us to Him.

GOOD THINGS

I say to the Lord, "You are my Lord;
apart from you I have no good thing."

PSALM 16:2 NIV

All good things come into our lives through God, whether it's a wonderful Christmas celebration or a lifelong dream.

What good thing could happen apart from God? Anything that is not of Him is sin, and therefore not good. If we engage in anything that is not His will, we'll soon find it breaking apart in our hands or destroying our lives.

If a much-desired dream has seemed to elude you, at least temporarily mark it "not good" in your mind. Perhaps someday God will bring it to you, and then you can plaster the word "good" across it and take it with joy. But today, God knows something you don't. Accept the goodness of that decision and know you can still live with joy.

Until your dream comes true or passes you by entirely, hold on to that really good thing in your life: Jesus.

SHARING HIS WONDERFUL DEEDS

I will give thanks to you, LORD, with all my heart;
I will tell of all your wonderful deeds.

PSALM 9:1 NIV

What wonderful things has God done in your life? Don't keep them to yourself. Share them with the world through a testimony of praise.

If a friend is going through hard times, don't just cynically reply, "Been there, done that." Tell the hope-filled story of how God was faithful in bringing you through challenges. If an acquaintance is doubtful about making a commitment to Christ, share the joy that salvation has brought to your life.

God has done wonderful deeds in every believer's life. We have a history of joy with Him as He has richly blessed us. Today, let's share that good news with others who need to be lifted up with hope.

A MATTER OF FOCUS

Let us run with endurance the race that is set before us, looking unto Jesus, the author and finisher of our faith, who for the joy that was set before Him endured the cross, despising the shame, and has sat down at the right hand of the throne of God.

HEBREWS 12:1–2 NKJV

How could Jesus give up heaven and come to earth to save us from our sins? We may never fully understand it, but we can always rejoice that our Lord saw the joy ahead instead of simply focusing on the pain. Where would we be if He'd balked at the suffering instead of looking beyond it?

Likewise, as we run our earthly race, we need to keep our eyes on Jesus, not on the troubles that lie ahead. Because before us lie not only troubles but also that throne where we will worship at Jesus' feet, awed by the One who foresaw this future glory.

JOY OF JESUS

Splendor and majesty are before him;
strength and joy are in his dwelling place.

1 CHRONICLES 16:27 NIV

When we feel bogged down by Christmas shopping, holiday plans, or maybe just the dullness of an overbusy life, we can get so trapped in trying to keep up with our schedules that our lives turn into drudgery.

That's when Christmas turns into a burden, not a pleasure. As joy slips out of our lives, it's as if we've temporarily stepped out of God's kingdom. After all, the One who has joy as His dwelling place would hardly appreciate a celebration of His Son's birth that brought so much misery.

Let's keep joy in our celebrations by focusing on the really important things. A larger tree with more ornaments on it isn't necessary. More shopping isn't imperative either. But focusing on the splendor and majesty of our Lord might be just what pushes our misery out the door.

This holiday, let's praise Jesus, and strength and joy will be ours.

GOOD NEWS

*How beautiful upon the mountains are the feet of
him who brings good news, who proclaims peace,
who brings glad tidings of good things, who proclaims
salvation, who says to Zion, "Your God reigns!"*

ISAIAH 52:7 NKJV

Like a messenger who carries news of a great victory
in battle, believers carry the joyful Gospel message
to the world.

Sometimes, when people turn aside from it, we
forget that what we bear is *good news*. Sharing the
Gospel has its frustrating moments, especially when
others tell us we're narrow-minded. But if they were
honest, they might recognize that they are the ones with
the narrow minds, since they won't even consider the
message.

The words we share today may not take root now.
But who knows when God will use them to light a spark
of faith in the rejecter? We cannot stop carrying the
message simply because results take time.

Keep walking with those beautiful, if dusty, feet. The
world needs to hear good news.

DELIGHTS OF THE SPIRIT

You satisfy me more than the richest feast.
I will praise you with songs of joy.

PSALM 63:5 NLT

We know what rich feasts are like at this time of year. Friends and family invite us to share a meal, church suppers abound, and office parties add inches to our waistlines if we're not careful. Though we may enjoy every bite and the fellowship that comes with it, we can quickly become sated with both food and conversation.

But one thing we never get tired of is the feast of Christ's love that is ours in this Christmas season. It fills every place in our hearts and minds better than food can fill our stomachs.

While we're feasting, let's not forget to fill our hearts with His love at church and at other gatherings. The delights of the spirit surpass the joys of good food and drink as we ask others to come to His feast.

RICH PROVISION

Command those who are rich in this present world
not to be arrogant nor to put their hope in wealth,
which is so uncertain, but to put their hope in God,
who richly provides us with
everything for our enjoyment.

1 TIMOTHY 6:17 NIV

Worldly wealth might allow you to take a sumptuous Christmas vacation and schuss down a mountain or lie on a sunny beach while others open more meager presents under a modest tree. But don't get too caught up in the wealth that allows you such benefits.

Wealth has its privileges, and at Christmas they may be more apparent, but riches only last for a time and can never feed the soul as communion with the saints will. Soon that holiday moment is no more than memories and pictures on a camera. Real joy lies in hope in the God who provides all things—whether a lavish vacation or a plain home in which to celebrate.

GIFT OF A CHILD

Children are a gift from the LORD;
they are a reward from him.

PSALM 127:3 NLT

*D*uring a hectic Christmas season, do you see children as a blessing or a disruption?

In so many ways, children are a blessing, especially because they delight so much in Christmas. Don't let the challenge of finding just the right gifts dim the joy of having a child to share the season with.

Spend time seeing Christmas through a child's eyes: the delight of a brightly lit Christmas tree or special ornaments that come out every year as a family tradition, the joy of a church Christmas pageant that shares the Gospel truth.

We all first come to Christmas as innocent children of the Father and see the brightness of His star. As years go by, that joy may dim. May children remind us of that first Christmas in which we knew Jesus was Lord of our lives and rejoiced at His gift of a Child.

ALWAYS ROOM
FOR THANKS

I will praise the name of God with a song,
and will magnify Him with thanksgiving.

PSALM 69:30 NKJV

Not only the angels praise God in song; humans do, too. But like David, many do so despite the troubles facing them. For in the verse before this, he laments, "But I am poor and sorrowful; let Your salvation, O God, set me up on high" (NKJV).

As it did for David, God's salvation can cause a quick turnaround in our emotions. We've been stuck in the center of sorrow, read a scripture verse, and suddenly been comforted. Or a friend has listened to us and shared Jesus' help in her own life, and our burdens have been halved. Seeing the power of God turns sorrow into rejoicing.

There is always something we can thank Jesus for, even on our darkest days. So let the praises begin, and send that sorrow on its way.

FULL OR EMPTY?

"He has filled the hungry with good things,
and the rich He has sent away empty."

LUKE 1:53 NKJV

Mary had never been rich. But the material things she missed hardly seemed to matter after the angel brought her the news that she would bear the Messiah. What wealth could compare to the favor God had shown her? This poor woman was filled with things the wealthy could never know.

God's idea of fullness isn't presents jam-packed under the Christmas tree, though it's nice when we have such things. A heart that's empty of Jesus remains barren even after all the gifts are unwrapped and the sumptuous dinner eaten. But someone who has Jesus and is thankful can be full no matter how bare the space under the tree (if there even is a tree) or how small the holiday meal.

Are we hungry for Jesus or for the other things associated with Christmas? Will we walk away full or with empty hearts?

O Come Ye to Bethlehem

WHAT'S IN A PLACE?

And because Joseph was a descendant of King David,
he had to go to Bethlehem in Judea, David's ancient home.

LUKE 2:4 NLT

When we think of the kings of Israel, Bethlehem isn't the first place that comes to mind. More often, we think of Jerusalem, that nation's capital city. Wouldn't it be more in order for Jesus to have been born there than in this relatively unimportant town?

Jesus' earthly parents traveled to Bethlehem because that's where King David originally came from, and Joseph was a descendant of David. As the couple obeyed the Roman command to head to Joseph's hometown, they fulfilled Micah 5:2, which foretold that the Messiah would be born in Bethlehem.

As the couple traveled, they may not have realized that their journey would identify Jesus as the One whom God had sent. But their obedience to both Rome and God identified their child as His Promised One.

Who knows where our own obedience will lead us?

TREASURES IN
SMALL PLACES

So Samuel did what the LORD said, and went to Bethlehem. And the elders of the town trembled at his coming, and said, "Do you come peaceably?"

1 SAMUEL 16:4 NKJV

The prophet Samuel had followed God's command and traveled to Bethlehem to crown a king. If God hadn't specifically called on him to go there, Samuel probably wouldn't have headed in this town's direction. And the welcome he got from the elders probably didn't encourage him to stay long.

But when he came to Jesse's household, Samuel found David, the young man God had called to lead His people, who would become a powerful king and a man after God's own heart (Acts 13:22).

God often finds great treasures in small places, perhaps even in places as small as our hearts. Just as a small town with a faithful shepherd boy became a place for the birth of His Son, our hearts can become important places for Him too, if, like David, we courageously welcome God's will in our lives.

ONE SMALL DECISION

Then Joseph her husband, being a just man,
and not wanting to make her a public example,
was minded to put her away secretly.

MATTHEW 1:19 NKJV

When we think of the Christmas story, most often we remember the positive side: the baby safely delivered and lying in a manger, angels singing of the birth, shepherds worshipping.

How often do we consider the trauma this birth caused Joseph and Mary? Joseph spent a short time thinking his faithful bride had betrayed him and pondered setting her aside. Mary probably feared being divorced before she was even officially married. The Christmas story includes a distinct element of sacrifice for the couple who made it possible.

But faithful Joseph listened to God and trusted that Mary had done no wrong; so Jesus was born in the right place and into a solid family. One man's decision touched the whole world, making sure the prophecy of Jesus' birthplace would be fulfilled.

What single choice of ours could help change our world?

A LARGE PURPOSE

"And she will bring forth a Son, and you shall call His name JESUS, for He will save His people from their sins."

MATTHEW 1:21 NKJV

When the angel told Joseph not to fear marrying Mary, he gave this confused man more than just mere facts. He gave hope. This child had a large purpose: saving people from their sins. And Joseph was to be part of that.

As Joseph bowed to God's will, it's unlikely Jesus' foster father knew just how big that salvation would be. When the angel said "His people," the carpenter probably figured that meant the Jews. But through the apostles, God reached out through Jesus to the entire world.

God uses "small" people to do unexpected things. Will we stay small or head out courageously to do our Lord's will? Can God use us largely, or only in a modest way?

In part, where we go is up to us.

REDIRECTED LIVES

Now when [the wise men] had departed, behold,
an angel of the Lord appeared to Joseph in a dream,
saying, "Arise, take the young Child and His mother,
flee to Egypt, and stay there until I bring you word;
for Herod will seek the young Child to destroy Him."

MATTHEW 2:13 NKJV

After traveling to Bethlehem and enduring the birth, Mary and Joseph may have been looking forward to going home and settling into their married life. But an angel came and spoke these words that redirected their lives. What followed was a time of excitement and fear as the small family headed into the unknown. Then they settled in a strange land.

Like Mary and Joseph, we sometimes experience a sudden life change that could only come from God—something we may dread as much as we're thrilled by it. Like them, we can be certain God goes before us, preparing the way for our future. We never walk anywhere that He has not gone ahead of us.

DON'T BE AFRAID

But the angel reassured them. "Don't be afraid!" he said. "I bring you good news that will bring great joy to all people."

LUKE 2:10 NLT

Any baby brings joy to the happy parents, grandparents, and extended family. A child born to a royal family might bring joy to a nation, but what child would have all people rejoice at His birth? Only Jesus.

When strange shepherds came and told Mary and Joseph of the angel's message, their joy must have extended to the new parents. How encouraged they must have been to see God's promises coming to pass. Though the struggling couple had been removed from their home by a census and forced to travel at the most dangerous time for both baby and mother, they began to see God's larger plan.

No struggle that God puts into His people's lives is purposeless. There's always a reason behind it. As the angel said, "Don't be afraid"—of the stress, of the uncertainty, of the hardship. He may be bringing good news.

LOUD AND CLEAR

For unto you is born this day in the city of
David a Saviour, which is Christ the Lord.

LUKE 2:11 KJV

When the angel announced that Jesus had been born in Bethlehem, the city of David, he was giving a specific message to God's people. It was as if he'd just erected a billboard saying, "The Messiah has come!" because this part of Jesus' birth fulfilled the prophecy in Micah 5:2; He was born of the line of Israel's kings and in the place where God had foretold.

The humble shepherds probably weren't spiritual giants and doubtless didn't have a lot of godly training, but they got this message loud and clear: God had entered their lives in a special way, bringing salvation even to them, the least people of Israel.

That angel's message never grows old. We rejoice in God's love as much today as the shepherds did on the day of Jesus' birth. And however many Christmases we celebrate, the news continues to delight us.

COME TO THE KINGDOM

"But you, Bethlehem Ephrathah, though you are small
among the clans of Judah, out of you will come
for me one who will be ruler over Israel,
whose origins are from of old, from ancient times."

MICAH 5:2 NIV

Where would the Messiah come from? The religious leaders immediately knew where to send Herod when he asked that question, and they pointed him to this verse.

Wouldn't that information alone have been enough to get Herod to worship—instead of kill—Jesus? Shouldn't it have sent those leaders immediately to the spot? No, because Herod had a kingdom to lose, and these leaders could see their spiritual power sliding away. The kingdom of self overthrew the kingdom of God in their hearts.

Will we hesitate to worship Jesus because we might lose a kingdom of self and self-indulgence or our false spiritual comforts? Like these men, we know where to worship and how. Will we cling to our tiny kingdoms or reach for His kingdom and gain eternity?

BY ANOTHER WAY

And [Herod] sent [the wise men] to Bethlehem,
and said, Go and search diligently for the young
child; and when ye have found him, bring me word
again, that I may come and worship him also.

MATTHEW 2:8 KJV

Instead of sending troops, crafty Herod sent the un-suspecting magi to Bethlehem to discover where the new king was. Israel's ruler intended to use them to unearth this threat to his throne; then he'd wipe Him out.

These innocent men searched out their King and rejoiced. Then God protected them, telling them not to return to Herod. They faithfully slipped away in another direction and returned to their homes (Matthew 2:14), leaving the baby safe in God's hands.

Sometimes, like the magi, we find ourselves in a position where leaders manipulate us. But when we remain in close communion with Him, just as He did with the magi, He can protect us even from the wicked hearts of kings.

SHEPHERD OR WARRIOR?

"And you, O Bethlehem, in the land of Judah,
are by no means least among the rulers
of Judah; for from you shall come a ruler
who will shepherd my people Israel."

MATTHEW 2:6 ESV

Though Bethlehem was no large, impressive place, it would not be the least of Judah's towns, for who could call the place where the Messiah was born unimportant? Micah 5:2 seems to underscore the smallness of the place, but this verse also recognizes the importance of the King who would be born there.

Here Jesus is described not as a delivering Messiah, but as a shepherd. First He would bring good news to His people and direct them in the Father's way. Later, a time will come when the Shepherd becomes a warrior and conquering king (Revelation 19:11–16). Those who refuse the way of the shepherd will experience the sword of the conqueror.

Everyone eventually knows Jesus. We can first meet Him as loving Shepherd or as conquering and judging King. Which ruler would we rather know?

GETTING OFF TRACK

*After this interview the wise men went
their way. And the star they had seen in
the east guided them to Bethlehem.*

MATTHEW 2:9 NLT

Knowing they were near journey's end, the well-meaning magi stopped in Jerusalem, hoping to find clear directions to the birthplace of a king. But Herod had been less than helpful, merely sending them on their way to do his dirty work.

These wise men never intended to do wrong. Checking out the local knowledge had seemed logical. After all, if a king were born, wouldn't everyone know about it? Unintentionally, they'd gotten off track with God's plan; but since they probably didn't know much about Israel's leaders, that's not surprising. God didn't desert them. When they were ready to travel again, the star continued to lead them.

Like the wise men, we may unintentionally get off track, but it doesn't have to end our journey. Once we recognize we've turned to man, not God, we ask forgiveness, and He provides a star to light our way.

FOLLOWING THE STAR

*[The star] went ahead of them and stopped
over the place where the child was. When they
saw the star, they were filled with joy!*

MATTHEW 2:9–10 NLT

After the wise men gathered their camels and readied themselves for the last leg of their journey, they looked up and followed the star to the place where Jesus was.

Scripture doesn't tell us exactly how God let them know the journey was ended. But this time they had no doubt, and there were no evil kings to lead them astray, just a small family and the tiny child they'd traveled so far to see. With their doubts at an end, joy filled their hearts.

When we reach the place of God's salvation, like the magi, we simply know. God's peace rules our hearts, and joy overflows.

A TINY MIRACLE

"For God loved the world so much that he gave his one and only Son, so that everyone who believes in him will not perish but have eternal life."

JOHN 3:16 NLT

*E*ternal life, wrapped up in a tiny child, appeared one night in Bethlehem. On an unsuspecting world, God thrust the full meaning of His love and salvation. But at first no one knew the whole story.

Angels, shepherds, and wise men celebrated the birth, but none expected the mystery that God sent their way: a child born to die for people's sins. In a ministry of only three years, Jesus provided the whole world with a new message based on promises revealed long before Mary brought Him into the world.

In one timeless moment, God, eternity, and humanity came together. One tiny miracle in a small town without bright lights and palaces brought billions of people into relationship with the Maker.

Has this tiny miracle filled your heart?

HIDDEN MESSAGE

So the family went and lived in a town called
Nazareth. This fulfilled what the prophets
had said: "He will be called a Nazarene."

MATTHEW 2:23 NLT

Have you ever been able to find the Old Testament verse that Matthew 2:23 refers to? Don't look too hard—you won't find it. But that doesn't mean the Bible lies. Turn to Isaiah 11:1 (KJV), and you'll find "and a Branch shall grow out of his roots."

The name *Nazareth* didn't exist in the time of Isaiah. There wasn't a town called that anywhere in Israel. So the prophet could hardly have named the town directly. But the word *Nazareth* means "branch." God used that name as a hidden message for His people. Between Jesus' birthplace, Bethlehem, and Nazareth, He knew we'd get the message.

If people tell you the Bible isn't true, tell them to look a little closer and see the Branch predicted hundreds of years before the town was there.

GOOD NEWS?

Jesus was born in Bethlehem in Judea, during the
reign of King Herod. About that time some wise men
from eastern lands arrived in Jerusalem. . . . King
Herod was deeply disturbed when he heard this.

MATTHEW 2:1, 3 NLT

Wise men suddenly appearing from the east? What was going on in Israel? Certainly Herod must have asked himself those questions, and when he heard the answer, he wasn't happy. These magi had come to find the new king of the Jews. Only one problem: Herod was already king of the Jews and didn't relish competition. So he immediately started a hunt to find and kill this usurper.

Herod didn't appreciate that news any more than we like it when a change disturbs our nice, ordinary Christian lives. We don't enjoy it, and we may do anything we can to stop it from happening.

When God brings spiritual change into our lives, do we embrace it or seek to quell it? Will we rejoice in His good news or try to avoid change at all costs?

ULTIMATE SACRIFICE

But I, by your great love, can come into your house;
in reverence I bow down toward your holy temple.

PSALM 5:7 NIV

*B*ecause He loves us, God invites us into His presence in Bethlehem. But we don't make a one-time, short-term visit, like the shepherds in the Bible story. Instead, when we ask Him into our hearts, we come into His presence for eternal worship.

God isn't searching for people who visit a church and watch a nativity scene as entertainment, then walk away. He's looking for those who want to become part of the scene, forever worshipping the Savior sent by the Father.

Today, recognize that God's great love draws us to Him. Bow down and worship the holy Savior who came to earth to make the real ultimate sacrifice.

STAND FIRM

All these people were still living by faith when they died.
They did not receive the things promised; they only saw
them and welcomed them from a distance, admitting
that they were foreigners and strangers on earth.

HEBREWS 11:13 NIV

Have you had a really dreadful day and wished that Jesus might pick this day to return? How wonderful it would be to see Him in all His glory and know that earthly things were finished! But God won't choose the day to send His Son according to our most embarrassing or difficult moments. His plan goes far beyond small problems we won't even remember a year from now.

So when we come to the end of an awful day and eternity remains far off, let's be reminded that the heroes of the faith listed in Hebrews 11 never received God's promises during their lifetimes, yet they held firm in faith.

How much more do we, who have seen the Son born in Bethlehem, have reason to stand firm?

O Come, Let Us Adore Him

A WORD FOR THE DAY

And she brought forth her firstborn son, and wrapped him in swaddling clothes, and laid him in a manger; because there was no room for them in the inn.

LUKE 2:7 KJV

We spend months thinking about Christmas, preparing celebrations, making our spiritual lives ready for the big day. But nowhere in scripture is this day given a name.

Christmas was not celebrated in the early church, and later efforts to identify the birthday of Christ were all guesses, since scripture is silent on the subject. The name *Christmas* comes from the Old English phrase *Cristes moesse* or "Christ's mass," reflecting the medieval fondness for celebrating the holiday liturgically.

Whatever day Jesus was born on and however we celebrate this event, it does not change the meaning His birth has for our lives. Without Him as our Messiah, we would have no hope of reconciliation with God. No matter what we call it, Jesus' birthday changed the world forever—especially our inner, spiritual worlds.

WORTHY OF ADORATION

For you created my inmost being; you knit me
together in my mother's womb. I praise you
because I am fearfully and wonderfully made;
your works are wonderful, I know that full well.

PSALM 139:13–14 NIV

Some days, adoring God just seems like too much work. After all, don't we have a gazillion things to do before Christmas? Aren't our jobs way too demanding and our household chores too overwhelming? How could we possibly fit in worship time, too?

Then we look at one hand and understand the amazing work it is, with delicate bones that make us able to move in almost any direction. We comb back our hair and realize that God has counted every one on our heads.

Suddenly the God who came as a tiny baby seems much more awesome and powerful. Praise and adoration are no longer a chore.

Come, let us adore Him.

FALLEN CITY

*Because God's children are human beings—made
of flesh and blood—the Son also became flesh
and blood. For only as a human being could he
die, and only by dying could he break the power
of the devil, who had the power of death.*

HEBREWS 2:14 NLT

Why did Jesus have to come as a human? Couldn't
He have stepped into this world like a superhero
and wiped out Satan in a moment?

Of course He *could* have. But that simply would
have shown His own power. It wouldn't have changed
human lives from the inside out. To break the power
of death, He came as an innocent baby, lived perfectly
in our fallen world, and died without sin. As Satan
unjustly took the life He willingly gave up, sin fell like a
beleaguered city, without a shot being fired.

Jesus became flesh and blood for one reason: to
break the bondage of sin in our lives. Will we accept His
sacrifice and worship Him or remain under the power
of death?

HUMBLE JOB

The LORD is my shepherd; I shall not want.

PSALM 23:1 KJV

*B*eing a shepherd was a humble and messy job, and it was hardly a respectable profession. No parent hoped for shepherding as a career for a favorite son. Yet God describes Himself as a shepherd and respected shepherds enough to send them as witnesses to the birth of His Son.

Shepherds had to care for silly, weak animals. When ewes got lost and rams were threatened by predators, their caregivers tracked them down or defended them, often risking their own safety. Without that shepherd's help, the creatures would soon be in deadly danger.

It's the same for us. Without our shepherd, we quickly find ourselves neatly wrapped in Satan's jaws. Yet Jesus comes to us, silly beings that we are, and at His own cost pushes us away from harm and onto the safe path.

It's not a high-class job, but it's one He chose—one only He could do. Will we praise him for His sacrifice?

WORSHIP THE KING

[Wise men came,] saying, Where is he that is born King of the Jews? for we have seen his star in the east, and are come to worship him.

Did you know neither gift giving nor a large feast was part of Christmas in the earliest New England settlement? The Puritans didn't celebrate the day at all.

At Plimoth Plantation, Christmas was a regular workday. The Puritans, finding no biblical precedent for celebrating the day, considered it a human addition to religion and passed it by. In 1621 Governor Bradford rebuked some new immigrants for playing games while others worked—and from that time on, no one openly celebrated the day on the plantation. New England held to that tradition for centuries.

The Bible may not describe a Christmas celebration, but it does show us what to do. Like the wise men, we can worship our King. Whether we travel far or stay at home, giving Him His proper place in our lives is never wrong.

WORSHIP HIM

"Yours, O LORD, is the greatness, the power, the glory, the victory, and the majesty. Everything in the heavens and on earth is yours, O LORD, and this is your kingdom. We adore you as the one who is over all things."

1 CHRONICLES 29:11 NLT

After he'd gathered all his officials and explained the building of the temple to them, King David broke out into this wondrous praise that inspired his people. This was the God they were building for.

As we reflect on the tiny baby in the manger, let's remember we're also looking at the same awesome Lord. He's the same Word described in John 1:1–5, the God-man through whom all things were created.

Sometimes it's easy to make Jesus our best buddy, a slightly more-than-human being but someone who is a good deal less impressive than the Lord described in this verse. Though He *is* our Friend, let's not forget He's also our all-powerful Creator and Redeemer. Knowing that, let's draw near and worship Him.

THE TENDER LORD

See, the Sovereign LORD comes with power, and
he rules with a mighty arm. See, his reward is
with him, and his recompense accompanies him.
He tends his flock like a shepherd: He gathers the
lambs in his arms and carries them close to his
heart; he gently leads those that have young.

ISAIAH 40:10–11 NIV

The Lord we adore is powerful beyond earthly measure. Those who remain in rebellion against Him have great reason to fear a day of judgment when they'll have to account for not following Him. But to those who love and serve Him, this powerful being has a most tender side. When we hurt, he gathers us up and carries us, leaning us on His chest. When we need gentle care, like a sheep who has borne young, He takes us by the easiest way.

As we walk in His way, His strength protects us and His kind heart draws us nearer to Himself. Who wouldn't want to worship such a tender Lord?

TURNING AROUND THE BLUES

The LORD is my strength and my shield; my heart trusts in him, and he helps me. My heart leaps for joy, and with my song I praise him.

PSALM 28:7 NIV

Trust in God is a wonderful thing. When we depend on Him, no matter what our day holds, we feel the joy of our Lord's presence.

But on days when we need God's strength and wish we had a shield in front of us to deflect some arrows of discouragement, we may need to remind ourselves that joy and praise are not where this verse begins. The leaping heart David speaks of came after he needed God's strength, not before. Trouble came before the trust, and during trouble this psalmist learned that his Lord would always be there for him, so his heart leapt with joy.

When holiday dejections sap our strength, let's grab on to our Lord. With His strength and protection, we'll soon be singing along with the praise choir.

HOLY, LIKE GOD

Both the one who makes people holy and those who
are made holy are of the same family. So Jesus is
not ashamed to call them brothers and sisters.

HEBREWS 2:11 NIV

Jesus is not ashamed to call us His siblings.

As we ponder that thought, we may mentally step back, realizing how unworthy we are to be Jesus' brother or sister. How could we attain to the qualities of our older Brother, even on our best days? Wouldn't He secretly be embarrassed by our failures?

But Jesus has already made us perfect. Through God's grace, we share His nature already, though we only see glimpses of it here on earth.

Holy, like God: We could never deserve it. But He blessed us anyway. Let's appreciate that blessing by worshipping Him with heart and soul and by living holy lives that glorify Him.

Then we'll give Him no reason for shame.

FLICKING FLIES

When he had called together all the people's
chief priests and teachers of the law, he asked
them where the Messiah was to be born.

MATTHEW 2:4 NIV

Herod knew where to go with questions about religion. He went to the chief priests and those who taught the law. Though these men probably weren't real Herod fans, since he was only half-Jewish and a very violent ruler, they knew scripture well enough to have an answer at hand and told him what he wanted to know.

Even though they knew the details of His birth, none of these spiritual leaders who should have been awaiting the Savior started a Messiah search or a praise party. Instead they flicked Herod's news off as if it had been an irritating fly.

God tells us to always be watching and ready. Are we doing so? Will we be ready to behold the fulfillment of His promises? Or will His return find us flicking some modern-day flies?

GIFTS FOR THE KING

And when they had come into the house, they
saw the young Child with Mary His mother,
and fell down and worshiped Him. And when
they had opened their treasures, they presented
gifts to Him: gold, frankincense, and myrrh.

MATTHEW 2:11 NKJV

The wise men opened their hearts and pocketbooks when they gave generous gifts to the baby Jesus. These gifts befitting a king also had other significances. Frankincense was used to perfume the temple's holy of holies, the holiest place on earth—it showed that Jesus was divine. Myrrh was used in anointing oil and for embalming, foretelling His death.

Their gifts showed worshipful hearts, but they did more than that. They showed the world that Jesus was the One foretold by God in Isaiah 60:6, after the prophet foretold that Gentiles would come to the Redeemer's light.

Watchful Jewish hearts could have known Jesus was God's special gift, but few were looking for Him. They found what they were looking for.

What do we look for today?

PRAISE VOICES

For at just the right time Christ will be revealed from heaven by the blessed and only almighty God, the King of all kings and Lord of all lords. He alone can never die, and he lives in light so brilliant that no human can approach him. No human eye has ever seen him, nor ever will. All honor and power to him forever!

1 TIMOTHY 6:15–16 NLT

Jesus came once as a tiny, unthreatening baby. But when He returns, it will not be a rerun of that humble birth. Instead, in a moment, in the twinkling of an eye, He will be revealed in all the awesome power that is rightly His.

This is the culmination of the Christmas message, the moment toward which His whole earthly life pointed. He will be shown to be God before believer and unbeliever alike, with the whole world as witnesses.

Are we ready for that revelation? Let's get our praise voices ready now!

ADORATION ACTION

For where envy and self-seeking exist,
confusion and every evil thing are there.

JAMES 3:16 NKJV

Christmas is a wonderful time of sharing and love. But where good things are, evil also draws close. So it's not surprising that at Christmas it's easy to feel jealousy over things we don't get. When we see others receiving treasured gifts, it's easy to feel sorry for ourselves. Or when another mother's child gets the role in the pageant that our child would have liked, it's a challenge not to feel bitter.

Putting ourselves aside and being happy for the one who has been blessed may be difficult, but when we realize the dangers behind a jealous attitude, it's easier to set it aside. That's why God gives us this down-to-earth warning.

Real adoration of God may mean putting our actions where our mouths are and living out the commandments He has given us. It's not an easy choice, but with His help, we'll share deep love, instead of damaging other lives.

BLESSED IN HIM

Let the whole world bless our God and loudly
sing his praises. Our lives are in his hands,
and he keeps our feet from stumbling.

PSALM 66:8–9 NLT

Need help finding something to praise God for? Here's an idea: Follow this verse's advice and thank Him that your life is in His hands and that He never lets you stumble.

It's easy to get so caught up in this world that we forget the obvious or small thanks we could give God daily. As we grow in Christ, we become so used to our faith that we may not clearly remember the confused time before Jesus came into our lives. For some of us, these were childhood days, and our sins seemed rather small. But others of us clearly remember the serious falls that were daily parts of our lives.

Either way, let's thank Him that His hand was under us, keeping us from ending up with our faces in the dirt. How blessed are we in Him?

Christ the Lord

A STILL, SMALL VOICE

And it was revealed unto him by the Holy
Ghost, that he should not see death, before
he had seen the Lord's Christ.

LUKE 2:26 KJV

Unlike most Jews, who simply knew that God would send the Messiah someday, Simeon had a narrower time frame: God told him it would happen during his lifetime. So when the Spirit moved him, and Joseph and Mary walked into the temple carrying a baby, Simeon knew God's salvation was there.

Sometimes God speaks to us in the still, small voice of the Spirit. It may go beyond the logical sense we use for day-to-day decisions; we may even wonder if we heard God's voice. We're wise to be careful and make sure it is God and not just our wishful thinking. But when we recognize that God Himself speaks to us, like Simeon, we can confidently step out in faith.

Listen for that still, small voice. Get to know it in your daily walk with Him. The Spirit never leads us astray.

THE BEST?

*And they came with haste, and found Mary, and
Joseph, and the babe lying in a manger. And when
they had seen it, they made known abroad the
saying which was told them concerning this child.*

LUKE 2:16–17 KJV

The shepherds hurried to a stable, filled no doubt
with cattle, the natural barnyard smells, and one
seemingly ordinary, tiny baby with two parents tending
gently to Him.

It had to have been something of a comedown after
a sky full of glorious angels. One could hardly blame the
shepherds if they'd taken a step back and wondered if
they'd gotten it right. This seemed more like their working world than the birthplace of a king. Perhaps the
angel's mention of a manger gave them the clue
they were on the right track. They soon looked
their fill and began telling the world.

Sometimes God draws us into humble situa-
tions that hardly seem to reflect His glory. Will
we take the best from His hands, or demand
a chorus from angels first?

ONLY UNLIKELY

"For with God nothing will be impossible."

LUKE 1:37 NKJV

What an uplifting verse! It's encouraging when we're having a rough day or working on a difficult project.

But for Mary, who had just been told that she would bear the Messiah, those words had an even deeper meaning. God was doing a once-in-forever thing—placing His Son within her womb. What unvoiced questions she must have had, questions the angel never could have answered. As the heavenly being left her, her mind must have been overwhelmed.

Nothing in our lives will be quite like the role God chose for Mary. Compared to her "impossible," overcoming even our biggest hurdles only seems unlikely. While she raised God's Son, we raise more ordinary earthly children. And any pressure we feel on the job must be fleeting compared to her need to raise Jesus well.

If God empowered Mary to raise His Son, how easily can He handle our needs? Impossible is only relative!

PEACE WITH GOD

Therefore being justified by faith, we have peace with God through our Lord Jesus Christ.

ROMANS 5:1 KJV

What price would be too great to pay in order to have real, constant peace with God? No sense of guilt for wrongdoing, no distance between ourselves and our Savior—that would be bliss indeed. What wouldn't we give for that?

But sin's tentacles wrap tight around us, and our hearts are corrupted. So even though His justification has given us peace with our Maker, we struggle to maintain it. Every day we make new, difficult decisions to keep that quiet in our hearts, though the tug of sin attempts to lead us astray.

God sent Jesus to the manger and the cross for that peace. As we focus on His grace toward us, will we turn away from sin and toward the peace He has placed in our hearts? What *will* we give up? We can be certain peace will have some price.

BABE AND LORD

In the beginning was the Word, and the Word
was with God, and the Word was God.

JOHN 1:1 NKJV

His birth in David's city was simply the start of Jesus' physical life on earth, not the beginning of His existence. For long before that day in Israel, before time even existed, Jesus was. And He was God, not simply some larger-than-life being. For without being fully God, He never could have brought us into relationship with the Father, and we never could have felt that deep cleansing of salvation flood our souls.

This side of heaven, we cannot fully understand Him, small babe and eternal Lord. Nor can we quite comprehend what brought Him to earth to suffer on our behalf. But we can kneel before Him in awe and love. And that is enough for now.

UNFAILING LOVE

*All we like sheep have gone astray; we have
turned every one to his own way; and the L*ORD
hath laid on him the iniquity of us all.

ISAIAH 53:6 KJV

We don't always intentionally do wrong. Sometimes we make a decision that we expect to turn out well, and it just doesn't. Or we can't see far enough ahead to avoid a mistake. Suddenly we're in a mess with nowhere to go. Then God compares us to straying sheep.

But if we think we have nowhere to go when we stray, we're wrong again. We always have a safe place, because even when we were headed off in our own direction, giving no thought to Him, God prepared a way of forgiveness through Jesus. Even when we couldn't think ahead, He was doing it for us.

Though we seek to follow Him, on those days when we slip, we are still held in the arms of Jesus, who never fails to love us.

NO SHORT-ARMED GOD

"Was my arm too short to deliver you?
Do I lack the strength to rescue you?"

Isaiah 50:2 niv

No doubt the trip to Egypt and the years there were a challenge for Joseph and Mary as they took the child a long way, then lived with strangers. But the couple obeyed God to keep Jesus safe.

Obviously, God could have brought the family back to Nazareth immediately. His arm was not too short to protect His Son within His own nation. But God had a purpose, not the least of which was the fulfillment of the prophecy in Hosea 11:1 that he would call His Son out of Egypt.

In our own lives, when God doesn't seem to answer prayers or make our lives easier, do we remember that His arm is not too short to provide deliverance? Do we assume He lacks the strength to help? Or do we know He will do it in His own time?

NEVER FORGOTTEN

Praise the LORD. Give thanks to the LORD,
for he is good; his love endures forever.

PSALM 106:1 NIV

Having a challenging day and feeling lost about something to thank the Lord for? Then start simply. Praise Him for His goodness. For surely good things have come into your life since He entered your heart: friendships you never would have had unless you shared your faith with others, improved relationships because you learned how to love others, a richer life because you shared it with Jesus.

Then know that this goodness will not end, because God loves you forever. He never stops bringing good things into your life, even if you're living in a time of trial today. Who knows what good will come out of this challenging moment?

If you sing your Lord's praises, despite your troubles, your heart will lighten, too. He has not forgotten you and never will leave your side.

ETERNAL CLAIM

"My sheep hear My voice, and I know them, and they follow Me. And I give them eternal life, and they shall never perish; neither shall anyone snatch them out of My hand."

JOHN 10:27–28 NKJV

When we hear Jesus' gentle voice calling us into faith and we turn from sin and into His arms, we join Him not simply for a day, but for eternity.

If, as some people claim, Jesus was merely an interesting teacher, we'd be on shaky ground claiming a hold on eternity. Good teachers have no business claiming they can provide eternal life to anyone. So a man who made such a claim wouldn't be a good teacher but a charlatan.

You can believe Jesus gives eternal life and trust in Him, or you can deny His claims to be God, but you can't claim He's not God and expect to gain heaven. His sheep know His voice, and He knows His sheep, but the goats don't hear His voice at all.

GOD'S TRUTH

And was there until the death of Herod: that it might
be fulfilled which was spoken of the Lord by the
prophet, saying, Out of Egypt have I called my son.

MATTHEW 2:15 KJV

When Joseph, Mary, and Jesus returned to their homeland, it must have been a day of celebration for the family. Finally they could return to Nazareth, see their family and friends, and worship in their own synagogue. Familiar things were returned to them again.

Though God gave joy to them in that move, He gave an even greater joy to the whole world. God fulfilled Hosea 11:1 by calling His Son out of Egypt, proving that Jesus was the Messiah Israel had long waited for. Through this and other Old Testament prophecies He fulfilled, Jesus proved He was who He claimed to be.

We believe Jesus is the Messiah not on a whim, but because He fulfills those prophecies. Our faith is true not because we imagine it to be, but because God's truth has proved it.

MORE THAN A GIANT

And there shall come forth a rod out of the stem of Jesse,
and a Branch shall grow out of his roots: and the spirit
of the LORD shall rest upon him, the spirit of wisdom
and understanding, the spirit of counsel and might,
the spirit of knowledge and of the fear of the LORD.

ISAIAH 11:1–2 KJV

All Israel knew a spiritual giant was coming who would be born of David's line. Isaiah had predicted it many years before Jesus' birth.

Plenty of people would like to believe that Jesus' importance stopped with His speaking nice, inspiring words and doing good deeds. But verse 10 (NLT) won't leave it there; it also describes Him as "a banner of salvation to all the world."

Either Jesus is a real giant—the kind who is both God and man—or He is nothing. We can't have it halfway, because scripture won't allow us to.

The giants of human imagination are just that, imaginary. They can't save us from sin.

Only God's Son can do that.

A BETTER PLAN

"For the LORD your God is the God of gods and Lord of lords. He is the great God, the mighty and awesome God, who shows no partiality and cannot be bribed."

DEUTERONOMY 10:17 NLT

Sometimes, like children at Christmastime who want a special toy, we try to "bribe" Jesus to do things our way, trying to get our Best Friend to give us what we want.

When it doesn't work, let's remember that He's in charge of the whole world, not just our lives. As King of kings and Lord of lords (1 Timothy 6:15), He does what's right—for us and for others.

But there's an upside to our not getting everything we demand: Jesus truly is in charge of the results of His plans and brings good things out of all of them, even the ones we rebel against. In the end, we'll be heartily thankful He didn't follow along with our machinations.

When the Lord of lords loves you, He always has a better plan.

REVIVED!

The one thing I ask of the LORD—the thing I seek most—is to live in the house of the LORD all the days of my life, delighting in the LORD's perfections and meditating in his Temple.

PSALM 27:4 NLT

Wouldn't it be wonderful to be able to spend all day, every day, in church, worshipping our Lord and keeping our minds on the right path? We could celebrate one great, constant revival service.

People have long tried to separate themselves out for God by going apart. In their attempt to flee the world, they distinctly limit their exposure to it. But as hard as we try to avoid the world, it follows along with us; our own sin is never entirely separated from us. Nor could we be much of a world-changing witness to our Lord if we lived at church.

The good news is that we can live in God wherever we go when our attitude is one of constant worship. Let's bring Him wherever we go, and we will truly be revived.

FULFILLING THE PROMISE

Andrew went to find his brother, Simon, and told him,
"We have found the Messiah" (which means "Christ").

JOHN 1:41 NLT

How do we know Jesus is the long-promised Messiah?

We don't have to rely only on this proclamation of Andrew's. God wanted to be clear that Jesus was the One He sent, so He gave us a map: prophecies that foretold much about His Anointed One.

The Christmas story fulfills a number of predictions, including that Jesus would be born of a virgin (Isaiah 7:14; Matthew 1:22–23), the flight into Egypt (Hosea 11:1; Matthew 2:15), His birthplace in Bethlehem (Micah 5:2; Matthew 2:1), and the fact that He'd be a descendant of David (Psalm 132:11; Matthew 1:1). Through His life and death, Jesus fulfilled many proofs that He was the man God sent.

No human could have arranged Jesus' life so it fit all of scripture's prophecies. Only God could bring everything together to fulfill the promise of His Son.

So don't hesitate to believe!

UNJOLLY HOLIDAYS

*She saith unto him, Yea, Lord: I believe
that thou art the Christ, the Son of God,
which should come into the world.*

JOHN 11:27 KJV

When her brother died, Martha's faith didn't fail. She made this declaration to Jesus, describing her trust in Him. But that didn't mean her heart stopped hurting at the loss of her brother. As mourners came to her home, even the wonderful truth that she would see him again one day seemed pretty bare. This faithful woman couldn't understand why Jesus hadn't come to her aid when she needed it most.

That emotion may be reflected by today's Christian who is suffering. Faith is not gone, but hearts can feel especially empty during the Christmas season. Holding on to hope seems barely possible.

As Christians, let's treat such folks tenderly but not invasively. We can acknowledge their suffering without trying to make them feel jolly and can give gentle comfort as our greatest gift. That may give the very hope they need.

REALLY BELIEVE

And they said, Believe on the Lord Jesus Christ,
and thou shalt be saved, and thy house.

ACTS 16:31 KJV

*I*f you had to encapsulate the message of Christmas in a few words, could you find a better verse than this one? Faith is what Christmas is all about.

At this season, you may see a sign that says "Believe." But believe in what? The sign won't define what's required for faith. And what it's talking about is probably faith in Santa, not the Lord Jesus.

None of the enjoyable things surrounding Christmas celebrations are its message. Santa or even angel ornaments on our trees cannot take the place of the real truth behind the holiday. Even nativity scenes may not draw us into God's truth, if they or we fail to focus on the real One the holiday glorifies.

Let's focus on Christmas's real center—the Lord Jesus, who came to earth for us. Then we'll know how to *really* believe.

ALWAYS LOVED

No power in the sky above or in the earth
below—indeed, nothing in all creation will
ever be able to separate us from the love of God
that is revealed in Christ Jesus our Lord.

ROMANS 8:39 NLT

Even the fact that Jesus came down to earth for us may not quite convince us of His love when we are feeling sad and sorry for ourselves. On days like that, our emotions try to convince us that when life is negative He no longer cares.

But the truth is that nothing separates us from God's love. If we're worn out from too much Christmas shopping or preparation for that special event, it's not God giving us a message—it's our bodies telling us we need a rest. If difficult relationships are tiring us out, it's not God forgetting about us.

The things of this world may irritate us, but they cannot stop God's love. Our Lord promised to love us always, and His promise never changes.

THE PROMISE REMAINS

For a child is born to us, a son is given to us.
The government will rest on his shoulders. And
he will be called: Wonderful Counselor, Mighty
God, Everlasting Father, Prince of Peace.

<small>ISAIAH 9:6 NLT</small>

When Judah faced dark times, the prophet spoke of One who was coming, a newborn child who portended hope for the nation.

None of the rulers of Judah in that day fulfilled the promise of Isaiah 9:6. And when the nation was taken into captivity, the powerful king of Assyria didn't fulfill it either. Judah looked far ahead to see God's promise fulfilled.

Of course, Jesus is the One the prophet foretold. But though we've seen certain parts of this promise fulfilled, we still look ahead to see the Wonderful Counselor, Mighty God, Everlasting Father, and Prince of Peace ruling our world. The fulfillment of that promise, which God will enact in His own time, lies ahead.

Still, we've seen the child of the promise and have good reason to believe.

THE BIG BOX

For the wages of sin is death, but the gift of
God is eternal life in Christ Jesus our Lord.

ROMANS 6:23 NIV

Some Christmas mornings, under the tree, you see a really big gift. Chances are that all eyes are glued to it until the tag is read. Maybe it's the first gift that's opened—or the last one, if the giver wants to hold on to the suspense. Either way, it's important.

This promise of God's gift of eternal life is the big box in our spiritual lives. We've been released from death into eternal life with Christ our Lord, who is the center of our world now.

But we've become so used to this verse, we may no longer think of it as a big box. Familiarity has bred contempt for it, and we can quote the verse backward and forward, forgetting what it was like when death was our payment in life. Let's remind ourselves of how we got this greatest gift and appreciate it fully.

True God of True God
VERY GOD

We know also that the Son of God has come and has given us understanding, so that we may know him who is true. And we are in him who is true by being in his Son Jesus Christ. He is the true God and eternal life.

1 JOHN 5:20 NIV

Jesus is God, or as the Nicene Creed says, "Very God of Very God." Though we cannot fully understand this mystery, over and over scripture shows us its truth, saying that eternal life comes only through Him and that Jesus and the Father are one (John 10:30; 17:11, 21).

To human minds, this truth is unimaginable. We may ponder how it works. How much is God and how much man? Where does one end and the other begin? But as hard as we seek to understand, it remains God's mystery.

God doesn't require us to understand everything about Him, only to believe—and that's a good thing, or we'd never enter heaven.

GOD'S MYSTERY

*Beyond all question, the mystery from which
true godliness springs is great: He appeared in
the flesh, was vindicated by the Spirit, was seen
by angels, was preached among the nations, was
believed on in the world, was taken up in glory.*

1 TIMOTHY 3:16 NIV

God's mystery is not a matter of figuring out who stole an impressive set of jewels or who killed another person. And Miss Marple or Sherlock Holmes could never work out how this event happened.

The mystery of God is that Jesus came to earth as a human to bring us salvation. We can never explain how God takes fallen people and makes them godly, though we have experienced it in our own lives. It's a miracle that we accept gladly and feel blessed by throughout our lives.

Mystified as we may be, let's not forget to be thankful and worship the Lord who offers His eternal grace. We don't need the solution to this mystery to appreciate the change it has made in us.

CHRISTMAS GIFT

He will cover you with his feathers. He will shelter you with his wings. His faithful promises are your armor and protection.

PSALM 91:4 NLT

This is the kind of tender love God gives to His people. Like a mother bird protecting her chicks, He hides us beneath His wings.

But how, you may ask, *can He do that? I can't get close to God physically! It's not as if He's standing next to me.*

We cannot reach out and take God's hand, but when we read His Word of truth and follow in His way, we snuggle under His wings. Nothing can harm us when we draw close to our Lord in spirit. To give us that protection, Jesus gave His life.

Compared to what He's given us, offering Him a Christmas gift of reading a few daily Bible verses is pretty simple, isn't it?

ONLY TRUE GOD

"And this is eternal life, that they may know You, the only true God, and Jesus Christ whom You have sent."

JOHN 17:3 NKJV

What's better than knowing "the only true God"? The best romance in the world can't equal that relationship, nor can our love for even the most promising child. A fancy home or car doesn't come close. Much as we treasure these things, they are limited and earthly. Though we love our families, they're not perfect, as Jesus is. And physical things can't reach the places in our hearts that hurt. Though they bring temporary joy, we cannot drag them into eternity with us.

We've tasted a mouthful of the joys of eternity. And our Lord promised it's just the beginning. No other "deity" brings the life that Jesus offers. So why waste our time with any of them? He alone is true.

KNOWING THE TRUE GOD

But the LORD is the true God; He is the living
God and the everlasting King. At His wrath
the earth will tremble, and the nations will
not be able to endure His indignation.

JEREMIAH 10:10 NKJV

The true God is not to be denied. He does not tolerate worship of useless idols that seek to take His glory.

Jeremiah's description of God in this verse isn't very comfortable. Most of us would rather have a kind, gentle Lord—one more like Jesus. But God the Father and Jesus are one. We can't choose His gentle side and ignore the awesome power of the "Old Testament" God. In doing that, we're trying to bring God down to our size and make Him less threatening.

Though God *is* gentle and loving, He does not tolerate idolatrous lies that draw people away from Him. Nothing that is untrue will stand before the true God, for truth is His very nature.

Do you know the *true* God?

WORTH IT?

But we do see Jesus, who was made lower than the
angels for a little while, now crowned with glory
and honor because he suffered death, so that by the
grace of God he might taste death for everyone.

HEBREWS 2:9 NIV

For a time, Jesus, the Word made flesh (John 1:14), was lower than the angels—God, humbled to the level of humanity.

Think about it in human terms, and it's hard to imagine giving up the glory of heaven for a hard lifetime on earth, a period of pain with the very modest gain of a handful of faithful believers. If we looked at it in profit-and-loss terms, the Son's efforts would hardly seem worth it.

But look at the great gain that came long-term: billions of people, through the ages, coming to salvation; souls saved throughout the world; a kingdom of redeemed people established by one sacrifice.

Worth it? Undoubtedly. Such huge eternal gains from short-term pain can only be a miracle of God.

TRUSTWORTHY GOD

*Every word of God proves true. He is a shield
to all who come to him for protection.*

PROVERBS 30:5 NLT

Do you know people who are trustworthy? Within
the best of their ability, they keep every promise
they make; their code of honor demands it. But sometimes, even with the best intentions in the world, they
can't do that. Life gets in the way.

But when God says He'll do something, we can
absolutely count on its happening—life can't get in the
way of the One who controls it. God is truth in every
part of His being, and as His Word, Jesus cannot be
other than true. So whatever He says or promises, we
can count on.

Jesus' truth often has earthly consequences
when people don't like hearing it. But though
battles rage around us, when we speak the truth
for Him, He faithfully stands by us. No word on
earth can change the truth of heaven.

If the battle is fierce, trust Him. He'll
always be true to you.

TRUE GOD

He led me to a place of safety; he rescued
me because he delights in me.

PSALM 18:19 NLT

Through all the centuries, no one has come up with a perfect explanation of why God cares for flawed human beings who, try as they may, seem to constantly fail Him. We can only be thankful that our true God sees value in us and decided to save us, though we had so little intrinsic value. Because He delights in us, He does not leave us helpless in a challenging world.

Not only does He love us, but He also rescues us whenever we're in trouble. Onetime salvation was not enough—He comes whenever His faithful children have need, even when we're not quite aware of it.

God is true to us even when we're clueless about our situation. He delights in us because it pleases Him.

How could anyone be truer than that?

MYSTERIES

By faith we understand that the universe was
formed at God's command, so that what is seen
was not made out of what was visible.

HEBREWS 11:3 NIV

Scientists have come up with some mind-bending theories of how life began. Yet as we read about their studies or watch TV programs that leave us with more questions than answers, we wonder how the Bible's teachings could ever fit with their ideas.

No matter how fascinating their theories, the book of Hebrews says that understanding creation is a matter of faith. For some, it's faith in science; for Christians, it's faith in God. After all, He alone was present when subatomic particles came out of nothing and were built into all we associate with reality.

The Lord whose birth we celebrate at Christmastime formed everything that was made. But understanding Him can be as much a mystery to us as how He created the world.

Some secrets God only shares with those who believe; others are His alone to understand.

TRUE FRIEND

The LORD is my rock, my fortress, and my savior;
my God is my rock, in whom I find protection.
He is my shield, the power that saves
me, and my place of safety.

PSALM 18:2 NLT

If we love faithful friends who stand by us no matter what, how much more should we love God, who provides us with a firm footing in life, protects us from harm, and saves us from sin? Even if we spent a whole day singing His praises, we could never thank Jesus for all His generosity toward us.

Though friends may share fun, faith, and challenges with us, they cannot compare to our Lord. When they can only listen, He provides solutions. When harm surrounds us on every side, He stands between us and hurt.

What truer friend is there than Jesus, who is both true God and true Friend?

NO RISK

"God's way is perfect. All the LORD's promises prove true. He is a shield for all who look to him for protection."

2 SAMUEL 22:31 NLT

No matter what He does, God always remains faithful. The Bible says there is no "shadow of turning" in Him (James 1:17 KJV).

Imagine, God does not have so much as a shadow that moves in shifting light. As the Light in whom there is no darkness, He cannot have one. We, who have cast shadows on the ground and done dark deeds since our childhood, can barely imagine what that would be like. In our earthly domain, we all rely constantly on the sun's light that causes shadows.

But in the bright light of the Son's love, there is no change or darkness. Though our sun might lose its power one day, Jesus cannot.

Relying on our sun might be risky, but there is no risk in relying on the Son.

TRUTH TESTIMONY

Anyone who accepts his testimony can affirm that God is true. For he is sent by God. He speaks God's words, for God gives him the Spirit without limit.

JOHN 3:33–34 NLT

The difference between God's people and those who don't know Him is usually fairly obvious. We know that God is true, and though doubts may sometimes plague us, we live in belief. Even when we don't intend to, we often testify that God is real.

At Christmas it's not hard to identify people who don't know the true God. Though we may love them and enjoy their company, we can see they have not accepted our testimony that Jesus is the One sent by God. Some refuse to have anything to do with the day; others just don't quite seem to get what it's all about.

This season, let's allow God to show His truth through us. Then as the Spirit works in the tender places of others' hearts and the truth fills their lives, they may find faith in Him.

PERFECT GIFT

Every good and perfect gift is from above, coming down from the Father of the heavenly lights, who does not change like shifting shadows.

JAMES 1:17 NIV

Just as God does not change, neither do His gifts. Whether they come at Christmas or another time of the year, they are always good and perfect. And if a gift is not perfect, we need to take a look and see if it really is from Him.

Perhaps that job that looked so perfect on the outside has begun to separate us from our family or require dishonest behavior from us; maybe we should look for something that really is God's will for us. Or maybe the new home we hoped to buy suddenly fell through; then we can count on it that God didn't intend for us to live there.

The gifts God gives fit into our lives well. Though we may face challenges in them, they will not destroy our lives or our faith.

That's a perfect gift from God.

Light from Light Eternal
LIGHT OF THE WORLD

When Jesus spoke again to the people, he said, "I am the light of the world. Whoever follows me will never walk in darkness, but will have the light of life."

JOHN 8:12 NIV

*I*magine living in a constantly bright, clear light, never having to squint to see clearly or even having to turn on a light. Everything around is easy to see.

That's the way it is spiritually once we know Jesus as our Savior, because His truths shine so brightly. When we walk with Him, even on our worst days, we can see far enough to take the next step. We constantly have direction for our lives. And as we look back on days past, despite the failings and challenges that come into our lives, we clearly see that the light of Jesus led us every step of the way.

His light never fails—and as we walk in it, we never need fear the darkness.

WORLDWIDE LIGHT

"The people who sat in darkness have seen a great light, and upon those who sat in the region and shadow of death light has dawned."

MATTHEW 4:16 NKJV

Centuries before Jesus came to earth, the prophet Isaiah foretold the coming of a great light reaching into the world's darkest places.

At the time of the prophecy, Israel was surrounded by pagan countries whose inhabitants believed that idols ruled in specific lands. Get outside one idol's nation, and they believed another god was in charge.

But Israel's Lord was not so limited. He created the world and ruled over all. And He cared about those who had never heard His good news. So when He sent His Son, God had Jesus set up His ministry in "Galilee of the Gentiles," and His message went out to the whole world.

God's compassion reached out with bright light to an entire hurting, ink-black world. What darkness in our lives could lie beyond its reach?

LIGHTS OF THE WORLD

*Ye are the light of the world. A city that
is set on an hill cannot be hid.*

MATTHEW 5:14 KJV

How can we be the light of the world? In our own power, we'd probably send out the radiance of one candle—or less, depending on how our lives were going. But when we're reflecting the Light of the World, His power cannot be hidden. Like a city perched on top of a hill, our testimony cannot be disguised.

God's light shines out of us even when we aren't aware of it. When we consistently obey Him, it becomes a habit to do His will. So we treat others with kindness, and the light shines into the darkness. We help a coworker because it's the right thing to do, and the light shines out again.

But when we recognize that God is using us as His lights, how much more effective we become; as we keep our lens clear to let Him shine through, the world sees Him ever more clearly.

LOVE THEM ANYWAY

If anyone claims, "I am living in the light,"
but hates a Christian brother or sister,
that person is still living in darkness. Anyone
who loves another brother or sister is living in
the light and does not cause others to stumble.

1 JOHN 2:9–10 NLT

These verses aren't scripture's most comfortable ones, because some Christians out there just make us crazy. Plenty of church members do irritating things: they have opinions that don't mesh with ours; they have habits that are less than perfect. . . . The list of irritants could probably fill a very large book.

God says none of that matters. We're still to love them.

That doesn't mean we have to feel warm fuzzies every time we see those folks' faces. That isn't what God's love is all about. It's the real "tough love" that cares for people even when we aren't fond of them.

Let's live in His light and love others, remembering that some of them have given us tough love, too.

SHINING OUT!

For you were once darkness, but now you are light
in the Lord. Walk as children of light (for the fruit
of the Spirit is in all goodness, righteousness, and
truth), finding out what is acceptable to the Lord.

EPHESIANS 5:8–10 NKJV

God made us light, but our spiritual story doesn't end there. We don't get to lie back on our child-of-light laurels and expect the world to give us glory. There's a job out there to do.

Children of light have been placed on earth by God for a reason: we need to shine for Him. As we search out His will for our lives and live for Him, we show forth the fruit of the Spirit. Instead of living in all kinds of filthiness and sin, we begin doing good things, standing for truth and reflecting God's light in our lives. It may be in small, daily things, but our lives start showing what good is. And people start noticing.

Suddenly the light is shining out in darkness.

JESUS' LIGHT

"No one, when he has lit a lamp, puts it in a secret place or under a basket, but on a lampstand, that those who come in may see the light."

LUKE 11:33 NKJV

As shy as some of us may be about sharing our faith, God tells us He doesn't want us to hide under a basket. He made us to shine brightly so that others will understand what it means to know Him.

That doesn't mean every Christian stands on street corners to spread the news. Some of us would cringe at that idea and be failures at it. But even quiet, unassuming Christians who hate to be the center of attention have gifts God can use to spread His Word. The soft, gentle gifts of caring for hurting souls may come naturally to quiet believers, and others may find it easy to bare their souls to them. A gentle spirit brings comfort to hurting hearts.

No matter what gift is ours, we can shine with Jesus' bright light.

LIVING IN THE LIGHT

Be kindly affectionate to one another with brotherly love, in honor giving preference to one another.

ROMANS 12:10 NKJV

What a wonderful world it would be if every Christian always communed with brothers and sisters as if they really are the important people God says they are—those who are loved by Him. But, being human, we don't always live in that truth. Instead of making others more important than ourselves, we may insist on our own way. The light of Christ may dim further as others respond negatively to our attitude. And soon the church that should have been the light on the hill is living in a pit.

But when we live in the light, putting others before ourselves isn't a threat, because we recognize that our own candles shine so dimly that they're barely seen. Only when Jesus shines through us can anyone see more than a mere glint of light.

But when we shine together with our siblings in Him, that powerful light reaches the world.

SILENCE THE CRITICS

Do everything without complaining and arguing,
so that no one can criticize you. Live clean, innocent
lives as children of God, shining like bright lights
in a world full of crooked and perverse people.

PHILIPPIANS 2:14–15 NLT

When the church is crooked and perverse, it sinks into the world around it and loses the testimony God meant it to have. Sin can't stand up and point the way to Him. Only those who live a Christlike lifestyle stand out in the crowd.

When we try to live for Christ, even when we do well, we'll easily hear the critics complain about Christian hypocrisy. They'll point out everything we do wrong. But we can't let that stop us, because even if no one commends us for having sterling testimonies, people notice when we start living right. And our small shining lights that reflect His light get their attention anyway.

Let's silence the critics by living out what we believe, and maybe those would-be critics will see the real Light.

NO EXCUSE

For ever since the world was created, people
have seen the earth and sky. Through everything
God made, they can clearly see his invisible
qualities—his eternal power and divine nature.
So they have no excuse for not knowing God.

ROMANS 1:20 NLT

Not only is Jesus the Light who shows us God, but He is also the eternal Light (John 1:1–5) that no darkness can overcome.

But that doesn't mean the darkness doesn't fight back. Those who turn away from Jesus have a bundle of excuses, and anyone who has witnessed to those doubters has heard them. Doubters think they have perfectly logical excuses for not coming to the Light. And they will air them at a moment's notice, often as soon as Jesus' name is mentioned.

But that doesn't mean they have a reason not to believe, as Paul points out. The world around them testifies to the Light. But they close their eyes, determined to remain in darkness—until the Light comes again and shines right through those closed eyes.

THE LIGHT WITHIN

"See to it, then, that the light within you is not darkness. Therefore, if your whole body is full of light, and no part of it dark, it will be just as full of light as when a lamp shines its light on you."

LUKE 11:35–36 NIV

*I*magine God's light shining through you, with no shadows or darkness. As every molecule of your being feels devoted to God, you experience the joy of His Spirit. God feels so near, and the fire of faith burns brightly within you.

That kind of fire is only an occasional experience, often followed by darker days.

Still, God doesn't tell us to live on a constant emotional high. Instead He calls us to let the light shine, unimpeded by darkness. Just as the lamps of Luke's day shone from one small wick, a little speck of brightness, our small lights can gleam constantly with the gentle glow of His Spirit.

No matter how low it burns, God's light remains within us. Let's consistently shine for Him.

THE ONLY LIGHT WE NEED

The city does not need the sun or the moon
to shine on it, for the glory of God gives
it light, and the Lamb is its lamp.

REVELATION 21:23 NIV

Though we're familiar with the idea that Jesus is our Light, that biblical truth doesn't mean we can turn out all the lights in our homes; we'd be standing in the dark. But one day, things will be different. We'll live in a city lit by God's glory, and Jesus will be our lamp.

What an amazing amount of glory that will take. What level of kilowatt hours could it compare to? If we were able to make a comparison, how much better would the light of Jesus be than anything this world can create? The light will be so powerful, neither sun nor moon will be necessary. There will be no night there (Revelation 22:5). Jesus will be all we need.

But then, He's always been that anyway.

SELF-CONTROL

*For the grace of God has appeared that offers salvation
to all people. It teaches us to say "No" to ungodliness
and worldly passions, and to live self-controlled,
upright and godly lives in this present age.*

TITUS 2:11–12 NIV

God's grace teaches us to live in the light with self-controlled, faithful lifestyles as we await our final salvation. It won't matter whether we leave earth for His kingdom or His kingdom comes during our lives. We'll avoid wrong and honor God.

Living in the light is not just a matter of feeling the Spirit fill our emotions. It requires us to make daily choices that deny the temptations that pull our hearts in other directions. As we choose to control our spirits and bodies, God's grace becomes apparent in our lives. That shining light encourages people of faith and draws unbelievers near.

When choices lie before us, let's remember we are not living for ourselves alone. Painful self-control today could lead someone—maybe even us—to glorify God's name tomorrow.

COMPLETELY SAFE

The LORD is my light and my salvation—
whom shall I fear? The LORD is the stronghold
of my life—of whom shall I be afraid?

PSALM 27:1 NIV

When we walk in a dark place while carrying a bright light, we don't fear. We can see where we're going, and any dangers around us become apparent as we walk along.

David tells us it's the same with God. When He is our light, our Savior, we know the safe way. He shines the light before us, and His protection keeps us from harm. But unlike walking on a dangerous street with a light, when we walk with Jesus, nothing can sneak out of a dark place and surprise us. This Light knows everything and cannot be surprised.

When we make Jesus our stronghold, there's no one we need fear. Nothing gets above Him, under Him, or around Him. We are completely safe.

OPEN THE LIGHT

Your laws are wonderful. No wonder I
obey them! The teaching of your word gives
light, so even the simple can understand.

PSALM 119:129–130 NLT

The laws of God are not rocket science, though their principles existed before the stars were hung in space. God designed His Word to be understood by everyone, even those without a lot of education or worldly advantages. He wants us to know what He expects of us.

Through His Word, God's light spreads across the world, to every kind of person. No one can plead the excuse that the message is too difficult to understand, though it is very profound. As the Spirit applies these truths to our hearts, we comprehend and obey.

Are we making enough of the light God sends us, or do we view Bible reading as a daunting chore? Let's open the Book and stand in His wonderful light. The more we read it, the more we'll see.

COME TO THE LIGHT

*The Gentiles shall come to your light, and
kings to the brightness of your rising.*

ISAIAH 60:3 NKJV

God's Word, the Law and the Prophets, had been given to Israel. And though there were hints that Gentiles would worship Him, most Jews pretty much ignored those clues in their own pride at fulfilling God's Law.

Then the magi, Gentiles who had no logical reason to search for a king in Israel, came asking where He was. It was a very upsetting day for Herod and all of his capital (Matthew 2:3).

If Herod had been more balanced, he might have rejoiced at the news. After all, he was no full-blooded Jew, and many Jews of his day looked down on him for that. Yet God prophesied that even Gentile kings could come to Him.

Jesus invites the weak and imperfect to come to His light (John 8:12). Will we join with Herod and be too proud to come, or will we seek the light that draws us to His side?

THE GIFT OF CHRISTMAS

But your iniquities have separated you from
your God; and your sins have hidden His
face from you, so that He will not hear.

ISAIAH 59:2 NKJV

Has the light of Christmas faded from your life? Maybe you're tempted to feel Christmas is only for children.

If that's how you feel, maybe you've never encountered the One behind the holiday, because the joy of knowing that God has separated you from your sins should never grow old. Or if you've met the Savior and Christmas has become old, maybe some old sin has slipped between you and the One who once seemed brand new and wonderful.

Don't let the gift of Christmas, Jesus, escape you because sin has hidden His face. Turn to Him and away from sin, asking His forgiveness, whether it's the first time or the millionth. He will always answer.

Find joy in Him, and the delight of Christmas will return. Sin destroyed is always something to celebrate!

UNNECESSARY STAR

"No longer will you need the sun to shine by day,
nor the moon to give its light by night,
for the LORD your God will be your everlasting
light, and your God will be your glory."

ISAIAH 60:19 NLT

Today we live in a world where the sun is all-important. Scientists tell us that without it, our earth would be destroyed. And we have no doubt that they are right.

But scripture tells us of a coming day when the sun will be unnecessary. God doesn't say what will happen to our universe's heat-giving star, but He tells us we'll have another light of such great brightness that it outshines our sun. He will be an everlasting light for us.

When scientists worry that the sun may explode and destroy us, we don't have to draw back in fear. Even if it does happen, we have a better Light—one that will never be destroyed. When our sun has long disappeared into oblivion, we'll be living with Him forever.

UNSTOPPABLE LIGHT

The light shines in the darkness, and the
darkness can never extinguish it.

JOHN 1:5 NLT

The light from the Word that John 1:1–5 describes reaches out into darkness, and as with the light of the sun, the darkness cannot overcome it. Imagine physical darkness trying to push back rays of light. It cannot; only when the source of the light is quenched can darkness overwhelm it.

Just as darkness has no hands to stop the light, Jesus' enemies cannot extinguish His brightness. No matter how many awful things happen in our world, the light shines with determination. No evil event can stop it; no human can hold it at bay.

Will the Light shine into our lives and push out the darkness? Only if we ask Him in and give Him access to every corner of our lives. When we open ourselves to the Light, He shines through us, and no darkness can eradicate Him.

Sing, Choirs of Angels
GOD'S MESSAGE

*Then the angel said, "I am Gabriel! I stand
in the very presence of God. It was he who
sent me to bring you this good news!"*

LUKE 1:19 NLT

Angels surround the story of Jesus' birth. Gabriel appeared to Zechariah before Mary heard the news that she would bear Jesus. He told the aged man of his coming son, who would have an important mission that supported Jesus' ministry.

In our popular view of angels, they are often airy-fairy-looking women who decorate our trees nicely. But Zechariah's angel was no frail being. Gabriel, whose name can be translated "strong man of God," stood beside God and carried out His wishes.

When Zechariah doubted this angel's word, he lost the power of speech until the birth of his son, John. It's not a good idea to second-guess God's messenger, and the Lord took Zechariah's attitude seriously.

When God sends us a message, whether or not it comes by an angel, will we take it seriously?

ANGELS BEFORE US

*As he considered this, an angel of the Lord appeared
to him in a dream. "Joseph, son of David," the angel
said, "do not be afraid to take Mary as your wife. For
the child within her was conceived by the Holy Spirit."*

MATTHEW 1:20 NLT

Angels flutter around the Christmas story well before they appear in the skies to share the message of Christ's birth. Even before Jesus was conceived in Mary's womb, an angel came to tell her the good news that she would bear the Messiah. Then Joseph got this heavenly word to keep him from divorcing the faithful Mary.

When we face questions in our own lives, we can trust that God has gone before us, too. Though no angel may appear before us, God guides and protects us as we seek to live for Him. Like Mary and Joseph, when we obey our Lord, we can be sure He will never fail us.

TRUE PEACE

And suddenly there was with the angel a multitude of the heavenly host praising God, and saying, Glory to God in the highest, and on earth peace, good will toward men.

LUKE 2:13–14 KJV

A piece of the glory of God came to earth that night to some common shepherds. One moment they were sitting watching their flocks. A single angel appeared; then a multitude of heavenly beings joined him in praising God. It was the most stunning event.

The angels' praise would have been fully understandable. After all, God was omnipotent, worthy of all praise. But peace on earth? While Rome ruled the rebellious nation of Israel and people probably complained daily about their rule? *That* was a novel idea.

God's peace on earth outdid anything the shepherds could imagine. His goodwill, shown through Jesus, influences every corner of believers' private, social, and spiritual lives. Suddenly, like the shepherds, we can glorify Him, believe in peace, and even share His goodwill toward others. That's glorious indeed!

THE MELODY IN
YOUR HEART

Be filled with the Spirit; speaking to yourselves in
psalms and hymns and spiritual songs, singing
and making melody in your heart to the Lord.

EPHESIANS 5:18–19 KJV

Angels are not the only singers among God's servants. Paul connects the filling of the Spirit with the joys of holy songs and tells us to share these tunes with each other.

A heart that's filled with Jesus is likely to break into a hymn in the most ordinary circumstances. And when that believer joins with others who are filled with praise, the music is likely to be one step from what we imagine the heavenly choirs to sound like.

Has the Spirit filled your heart with joy? Don't be afraid to let it out. Sing in the shower. Sing as you prepare a meal. Sing together with your family or with other believers. Let others hear the melody He has put in your heart.

MAGNIFY GOD

Let all those that seek thee rejoice and be
glad in thee: let such as love thy salvation say
continually, The LORD be magnified.

PSALM 40:16 KJV

*I*t doesn't matter if you're having a bad hair day, problems with the family, or a monster workweek. You can still rejoice.

Why? Because none of those transitory things affect your salvation. When your hair is going in the wrong direction, your kids are, too, and you can barely breathe because you have more work than any human could reasonably do in twenty-four hours of a day, God still loves you best. You're His child, and nothing changes that. Just because other things overwhelm you, He hasn't forgotten you.

Grab onto that truth, take a deep breath, and start singing with the angels. Nothing can keep you from His love, no matter what irritations pass through your life today.

GOOD COMPANY

The highest angelic powers stand in awe of God.
He is far more awesome than all
who surround his throne.

PSALM 89:7 NLT

Mary, Joseph, and the shepherds had never seen anything like the angels who gave them God's messages. They must have felt awed at these beings' appearance and the messages they bore. Certainly no one doubted who had sent them.

But angels, as impressive as they may be, cannot compare to their Lord. The awe we feel toward a mighty God is not ours alone. Even those who stand before him constantly and watch Him work out His purposes remain in wonder at His grace.

Though we seek to understand Him, God remains so beyond our finite minds that all we can do is bow in worship. When we do that, we're in good company—that of the angels who sang the Christmas news and of Jesus' parents, who accepted their role in God's work.

ORDINARY DAYS

Praise the LORD, you angels, you mighty ones
who carry out his plans, listening for each of his
commands. Yes, praise the LORD, you armies
of angels who serve him and do his will!

PSALM 103:20–21 NLT

After the angels delivered their once-in-eternity Christmas messages, they didn't cease to exist. They carried out God's will, continuing to sing His praises.

Nor did the birth of Jesus end Mary and Joseph's lives, though we know little of them after Jesus' early days on earth. Yet the couple to whom God entrusted His Son must have cared well for Him, for Jesus "grew in wisdom and in stature and in favor with God and all the people" (Luke 2:52 NLT). Though Mary and Joseph's important days moved on to ordinary days of faithfulness, even the least of those unreported days was important because they served God. Jesus grew up surrounded by love and faithfulness.

Like Joseph, Mary, and the angels, are we praising God by making our ordinary days important in service to Him?

JOIN THE ANGELS

Give thanks to the LORD and proclaim his
greatness. Let the whole world know what he
has done. Sing to him; yes, sing his praises.
Tell everyone about his wonderful deeds.

1 CHRONICLES 16:8–9 NLT

That angels should sing of God's glory seems quite natural. After all, don't they serve Him in heaven? They see His great feats every day. Why wouldn't they sing?

But the song doesn't end there, because angels are not the only ones who have seen the wonderful works of God. Humans have experienced something the heavenly angels have never needed: God's salvation and cleansing from sin. Only we have known the feeling of that load of sin dropping away and God's cleansing Spirit entering our hearts.

Even if you don't feel like singing today, you have reason to join the angels in praise. God's greatness connected with your life when salvation entered your heart. That's something to sing about every day.

HEAVENLY MESSENGERS

Therefore, angels are only servants—spirits sent
to care for people who will inherit salvation.

HEBREWS 1:14 NLT

Those glorious messengers who brought the good news of the Messiah to earth may have stunned the humans who heard their message, but Mary, Joseph, and the shepherds had nothing to fear. God sent the angels not to terrify, but to minister to these people for whom the child had come. Salvation was in their future because of the child whose birth the angels announced.

Our minds may struggle to understand that God sent beings from His very throne room to serve fallen humanity. Were the biblical people so much holier than we, that God would do such a thing? No, scripture tells us that all have sinned and fallen short of God's glory, and that's true of even the best of biblical people. God sent His trusted angels to share the most important news ever with the most ordinary humans.

Your own ordinariness may be the very thing that sent Him to you.

PROMISES KEPT

But you have come to Mount Zion, to the city of the living God, the heavenly Jerusalem. You have come to thousands upon thousands of angels in joyful assembly.

HEBREWS 12:22 NIV

Today may not be the most joyful day of your life. Perhaps a disaster seems ready to overwhelm you, or you just have so many chores, it seems impossible to get through them. Don't give up; there are better times ahead. Heaven and the blessings of faith still lie before you.

One day you'll join the angels in praising the Lord you served on earth. With the rest of the redeemed, you'll raise your voice, adoring the Lamb.

Though heaven may seem far distant today, recognize, as the writer to the Hebrews did, that its reality is very near. What God promised will come to pass, and you can be as sure of it as if it were in your life this moment.

God never fails to keep His promises. But now it's our time to keep ours.

All Glory in the Highest
LIGHT IN DARKNESS

Arise, shine; for your light has come! And the glory of the LORD is risen upon you. For behold, the darkness shall cover the earth, and deep darkness the people; but the LORD will arise over you, and His glory will be seen upon you.

ISAIAH 60:1–2 NKJV

Isaiah lived in a tumultuous time. The Assyrians had overrun most of the Middle East, and Judah was frequently at war. Much of this prophet's book is not pretty reading as he takes his people to task for their sin. But in the middle of all this trouble, Isaiah gave God's people the hope of His glory.

Rome was in a similar situation when God sent Jesus to redeem the whole world. And today's world doesn't seem to be any better, with sin hitting us in every corner of our world. But God still sent His Son to be our light. Will we shine in the darkness for Him?

CHRISTMAS LIGHT

Satan, who is the god of this world, has blinded the minds of those who don't believe. They are unable to see the glorious light of the Good News. They don't understand this message about the glory of Christ, who is the exact likeness of God.

2 CORINTHIANS 4:4 NLT

We share the Good News with a friend or relative, and instead of getting an immediate, joyous response, we receive arguments and rebuttals. The glory of Jesus that seems so obvious to us is clearly not even noticed by the one with whom we shared.

It's not necessarily that we said the wrong words or had wrong thoughts in our hearts. But Satan controls the minds of unbelievers so they cannot understand. The light that shines brightly for us is darkness to their eyes.

Instead of walking away in a huff, let's commit ourselves to prayer that may loose the enemy's hold on that heart and turn an unbeliever to the Christmas Light. Then it will shine brightly in another part of the world.

WAITING FOR THE LIGHT

*"For my eyes have seen Your salvation. . .a
light to bring revelation to the Gentiles,
and the glory of Your people Israel."*

LUKE 2:30, 32 NKJV

Simeon was an amazing man. Having seen the baby
Jesus, he immediately identified him as God's Messiah. Promised by the Holy Spirit that the Savior would
come in his lifetime, this devout man had been ready
and waiting.

Though every Jew knew the Messiah would come,
many hardly seemed to be looking for Him. Perhaps
such low expectations came from boredom with formal
religion or doubt that God really would be faithful.
Whatever the reason, many missed the news concerning
the promised child. He who was meant to be the glory of
God's people was simply ignored by many who should
have known better.

Like Israel, we have heard the promises. Are
we ready to see more that God will fulfill during our
lifetimes, or have daily burdens dulled us to them? Will
we see His glory fulfilled or miss it entirely?

NEVER-ENDING GLORY

Thou hast turned for me my mourning into dancing: thou hast put off my sackcloth, and girded me with gladness; to the end that my glory may sing praise to thee, and not be silent. O Lord my God, I will give thanks unto thee for ever.

PSALM 30:11–12 KJV

Most Christians don't have reputations as party animals, but that's because no one is looking at the right party. When believers party with Jesus, there is no risk of doing wrong or feeling awful the next day, so we don't have to shun a party because it would be harmful. Jesus' parties are pure rejoicing. Though an unbeliever wouldn't know what to make of them, the forgiven know that nothing is better than celebrating with the Lord.

When we delight in Jesus, there is no sadness; with our sins far away from us, we can sing His praises forever. With Him, the praise party never ends, and Christians know that's just the way it should be.

WORSHIP GOD'S MAJESTY

O Lord, our Lord, your majestic name fills the earth! Your glory is higher than the heavens.

Psalm 8:1 nlt

Consider God's glory. What is like it in the earth? Do great mountains or deep valleys teach us of their Creator? Does the glorious night sky tell us of His power? As beautiful, detailed, and impressive as the world God has designed is, it merely reflects His nature. Just as we humans barely compare to Him, so other parts of creation can simply point the way to the glories of the One who made them.

God's glory goes beyond our small planet, beyond the galaxies that came from His fingers. He is greater than black holes or magnetic space bubbles and more mysterious than "dark flow." Even these entities cannot describe His greatness.

Though we cannot understand Him, we can still worship. As we feel the awe surround us, we know that this glorious Lord loved us enough to reach down into our seemingly insignificant world and bring us to Himself.

A MARVELOUS SONG

Sing to the LORD, all the earth; proclaim his salvation day after day. Declare his glory among the nations, his marvelous deeds among all peoples.

1 CHRONICLES 16:23–24 NIV

God's glory is not something we're meant to keep to ourselves. When we know the incredible love He offers to all people, the wonder of it should burst from our lips and flow through our lives. How delightful to share the good news that the glorious Creator of our universe and galaxies beyond cares for every bit of our broken, dysfunctional lives and wants to remake them in His own image.

When our delight in God is a song, not a bludgeon that attacks others, they can be drawn to us and to our Savior. Instead of sharing His love through guilt or because it's a chore God has given us, we will sing of the marvelous things He has done—and then others are more likely to listen.

THE GLORY OF GOD

The heavens declare the glory of God; the
skies proclaim the work of his hands.

PSALM 19:1 NIV

If angels hadn't glorified Christ's birth with their songs, creation might have taken part in the joy. Even on an ordinary day, God's world speaks to all people of His power through its beauty and splendor. His glory is not something that can be hidden.

If it's true that you can tell a lot about people by their work, how much more does creation tell us of God's omnipotence? He who created our world made the delicate butterfly wing and the massive Alps. He filled the oceans with teeming life and created seemingly barren deserts that still hold creatures suited to their own environment. The heavens that declare His glory hold clouds, sun, and stars, all beautiful in their different ways.

Yet on Christmas, God did something even more glorious when He sent His Son to earth. Eternity wrapped in a tiny child, our salvation in physical form.

HIS GLORY

All have sinned and fall short of the glory of God,
and all are justified freely by his grace through
the redemption that came by Christ Jesus.

ROMANS 3:23–24 NIV

Humanity, for all its wonders, falls far short of God in His glory. His perfection is besmirched by our human inability to always get things right, even when we're trying to do so. Like a child who hasn't quite developed the physical dexterity to color in between the lines, we irritatingly scribble in places we shouldn't. Sometimes we even do it intentionally, with bitter spirits. We aren't always nice children.

Yet for all our inability to do right, God does not give up on us or let us destroy our own environment and that of others. Instead, He gave us a human-sized example we can understand: Jesus.

As we learn from Jesus, we see where we've colored outside the lines. Soon we begin to give up scribbling for the design He shows us. Then we appreciate His glory in our lives.

GREAT AND GLORIOUS

*It pleased the LORD for the sake of his righteousness
to make his law great and glorious.*

ISAIAH 42:21 NIV

Maybe we think of God's law as a book of rules
and regulations, as the reason we can't engage in
some fun things that God doesn't allow, or as something
we rebel against at times when sin clouds our vision. If
we think that way, we've bought Satan's lie, because God
describes His law as great and glorious, something that
flows out of His own righteousness.

Through this law, we've come to know God, been
told of His past acts, and learned about Jesus. Without
God's Word, we'd live in ignorance, missing out on the
prophetic promises God gave concerning His Son. We
wouldn't be quite so sure Jesus is whom he claimed
to be.

Let's celebrate the greatness and gloriousness of
God's Word and appreciate His work in our lives
through it.

THE GLORY
OF GOD

*For God, who said, "Let there be light in the
darkness," has made this light [of the Gospel]
shine in our hearts so we could know the glory
of God that is seen in the face of Jesus Christ.*

2 CORINTHIANS 4:6 NLT

nowing God's glory can be a scary thing. The Lord
of all has power beyond all we can imagine—but
what we can imagine is scary enough!

God wanted to share His light with us, so He gave
it a face we could relate to and love: Jesus. While we
might look at the power of the Father and fear, when
we think of Jesus, we see the sacrifice of His love.
Though we know He is the almighty God, we also
see His kind face, dispelling our fear. Love and glory
combine in one Man.

The same God, the same love. Our one true Lord
reaches out to us with light He yearns to share and that
fills our hearts with joy.

GLORY AND HONOR

*What are mere mortals that you should think
about them, human beings that you should care for
them? Yet you made them only a little lower than
God and crowned them with glory and honor.*

PSALM 8:4–5 NLT

What glory could we boast of, compared to God's? Yet despite our limitations and failures, God has crowned us with a small measure of glory and honor. Not the glory given to His Son, but that of rulers of the world He created. We could never take the place of our Lord, but we can be in charge of His earth, under His authority (Psalm 8:6–8). That's an awesome responsibility.

As earth's rulers, humanity has often failed, as evidenced by the state of our world. Instead of being God's stewards, people have often been greedy and used the earth for their own purposes.

So when we recycle bottles and cans or make sure a stream is not polluted, let's remember who we're doing it for and appreciate the glory of His world.

NO OTHER OPTION

*"And now, Father, glorify me in your presence with
the glory I had with you before the world began."*

JOHN 17:5 NIV

As Jesus neared the end of His life on earth, He prayed to be returned to the glory that had been His in heaven. If anyone doubts His claim to deity, this verse, which clearly describes Him as being with the Father before the creation, ends all questions.

From the time He was a small child being visited by strange kings and shepherds, with a star above His cradle, only one truth was proclaimed: This is the Son of God, the foretold Messiah, God's Anointed One. Anyone who claims any less is reading another book or intentionally ignoring the testimony of the scriptures.

The Son cannot be separated from His testimony and the prophecies of the Law and the Prophets. We accept His right to glory, or we deny Him completely.

There is no other option.

CONSTANT PRAISE

I will sing to the LORD as long as I live.
I will praise my God to my last breath!
PSALM 104:33 NLT

Giving God the glory isn't a onetime thing for Christians. We don't praise Him on the day He comes into our lives and saves us, then leave our praise songs on the shelf.

Every day God does something wonderful in our lives. He reveals new truths to us in His old Word; He guides us in the path we should take each morning and keeps us safe through the night. Whenever we face a challenge and wonder what we should do, He gives us the wisdom to walk in His path.

Do we praise Him for every way He helps us? Or do we just expect Him to know how much we appreciate His help?

The psalmist recognized how much he owed to God and showed his appreciation constantly. We'd repeatedly thank a human who helped us, wouldn't we? How can we do less for our Lord?

CHORUS OF PRAISE

You are my God, and I will praise you!
You are my God, and I will exalt you!

PSALM 118:28 NLT

What gets exalted in our lives? Is it our work, our family, or our activities? What do people know about us? What do we talk about? How do we live?

All those things can tell others what has first place in our lives. We don't have to witness to people until they want to run away from us. No one appreciates having a Bible waved before them constantly. But when we live consistently for Jesus, as well as share His Word, His truths become apparent to others, and they can be drawn to the One we exalt in our lives.

How we live 24/7 is as much a part of our testimony as the scripture verses or experiences we share. Our whole lives should praise our Lord and be a message to the world. Then others can see His light shining through us and come to join in the chorus of praise.

ETERNAL HAPPY ENDING

Behold, the days come, saith the LORD, that
I will raise unto David a righteous Branch,
and a King shall reign and prosper, and shall
execute judgment and justice in the earth.

JEREMIAH 23:5 KJV

Wonderful as it is, the Christmas story is not the end of the story. It is only a delightful beginning that leads to the ministry and sacrifice of Jesus, through His resurrection, to the spread of the good news of salvation to all humanity.

But the end of the story has only been hinted at in scripture. One day our Messiah will come to exact God's justice on earth as it has never been seen before. For those who do not know Him, this will be a sorrowful time of retribution. But for those who love Him, it will be a delight, because no matter what happens, we will be with Him.

Finally, in eternity, we will live with and delight in our Savior forever—the eternal happy ending. Are we ready for that day?

HAPPY CHRISTMAS

Devote yourselves to prayer with an
alert mind and a thankful heart.

COLOSSIANS 4:2 NLT

Is prayer part of our Christmas, or does it just go out the door when sleigh bells start ringing? Do we use the season to devote ourselves to communication with our heavenly Father?

This time of year, it's easy to get so caught up in our own plans and daily business that we hardly have time for our Lord. Though He is the center of the season, until we've finally opened the gifts, eaten the dinner, and said good-bye to much-loved guests, we may not take time for more than a quick word of thanks before our elaborate meal.

Instead, let's celebrate the holiday with an alert mind and thanks for the Savior whom we celebrate. Maybe we can take time before opening gifts to thank the Giver for the greatest Gift of all.

When we keep Him at the celebration's center, we'll have a happy Christmas.

FOR GOD'S GLORY

*So whether you eat or drink, or whatever
you do, do it all for the glory of God.*

1 CORINTHIANS 10:31 NLT

With all the food and drink that are a part of Christmas celebrations, it's hard to avoid over-indulgence. Often we end the season feeling sorry for ourselves because we've added pounds to a body that didn't need them. Others may have had things to drink that weren't good for them and may pay the price, too.

No matter what we do during this holiday, we should remember to do it to God's glory. Though the Corinthians debated over food or drink offered to idols, and we need to consider whether we've made what we put in our mouths an idol, the principle is the same: Our lives should glorify the One who made the food, not those who eat it.

So whatever we eat or drink, let it glorify God and not humans, even when they've made the most "heavenly" looking desserts!

ALL GLORY IN THE HIGHEST

. . .on the day he comes to be glorified in his holy people and to be marveled at among all those who have believed. This includes you, because you believed our testimony to you.

2 Thessalonians 1:10 NIV

Imagine Jesus returning to earth with His angels, righting every wrong done to Christians and punishing those who have denied Him. That's not a scene from a B movie, but a prophetic promise from the apostle Paul as he speaks of Christ's Second Coming (2 Thessalonians 1:5–9).

We will reflect His glory, even as we marvel at Jesus' coming. All we have believed for so long will become apparent as He stands before us in His glorious power. Without a second thought, we'll give Him "all glory in the highest."

But why save up all that praise for the moment He comes in power? We know His claims are true, though we "only" do so in faith. Yet isn't faith what it's all about?

Let's start the praising now.

CHRISTMAS DEEDS

*What good is it, my brothers and sisters,
if someone claims to have faith but has no
deeds? Can such faith save them?*

JAMES 2:14 NIV

Christmas is *the* time for goodwill in the Christian calendar. Even the most Scrooge-like person gets a gift in the office gift exchange, and most people feel a sudden concern for the less fortunate. All that is good. Scripture calls us to do good deeds.

But let's not leave that goodwill behind as the holiday slips behind us. Instead, let's bring that goodwill into the new year. That doesn't mean we must hand out gifts all year long, but perhaps we need to give the office Scrooge a break and stop the gossip about him, and maybe we need to be part of church missions that care for others all year long. Or God may show us others in our lives who need our help.

Then we will have been faithful for more than just one month, and God will be glorified.

ACCEPTABLE?

The angel went to her and said, "Greetings,
you who are highly favored!
The Lord is with you."

LUKE 1:28 NIV

Scripture gives us no indication that Mary was perfect. Like any mother, she worried when young Jesus disappeared and later when He began a dangerous ministry. With other family members she even tried to convince Him to draw back from His mission.

At Jesus' birth, Mary needed God's blessing and strength for the task before her. But God saw something in her that she may not have seen in herself: the faith and tenderness of a good mother.

Like Mary, we are less than perfect, yet God still calls us to service for Him. He favors us with His love and work that glorifies Him. He remains with us as we strive to carry out His will.

Let's not ignore the plans God has for us, in fear that we are not acceptable. Instead, let's return His favor with a life that gives Him alone the glory.

GLORIFIED WITH GOD

*The Spirit Himself bears witness with our spirit that we
are children of God, and if children, then heirs—heirs
of God and joint heirs with Christ, if indeed we suffer
with Him, that we may also be glorified together.*

Romans 8:16–17 nkjv

When the Bible calls on us to glorify God, it's
not because He is like a human who is stuck
on himself. As our Creator and Savior, He is completely
worthy of all praise.

That doesn't mean we are worthy of glory. Yet God
makes us heirs with Jesus and gives us the opportunity
to be glorified with the One who suffered for our sin. We
don't even deserve salvation, and we could never repay
all Jesus has done for us. How incredible it is to know
that by suffering with Him, we can be glorified with the
Savior.

That gives us a whole new perspective on the person
who dubbed us "preacher" or the job lost because we
refused to lie, doesn't it?

OUR GLORY
PROFILE

*O God, we give glory to you all day long and
constantly praise your name.*

PSALM 44:8 NLT

Constant praise? When would we have time to work,
care for our families, and do the myriad of things
required of us in a single day while we did this? How can
God expect it of us?

We all have an underlying current to our days, an
attitude that's there whether we're working in the office,
driving the kids to school, or doing laundry. Is it one of
complaint or faith? Do we think of Jesus or the problems
of our day in the moments when our minds are not
engaged?

If we take a look at our underlying attitude and find
it praise filled, and our intentional thoughts focus on
God's will as much as possible, we are giving Him glory
and constantly praising Him. If not, prayer and praise
can change our glory profile. When we make them
habits, they'll be there to stay.

GLORIFY HIS NAME

With all my heart I will praise you, O Lord my
God. I will give glory to your name forever.

PSALM 86:12 NLT

Praise is a very personal thing because God works
in every heart in a different way. Each of us has a
special praise to offer, based on how God has worked
in our lives. Some of us thank Him for forgiving us and
helping us overcome powerful temptations, while others
praise Him that our lives have sailed much calmer seas.

No matter what kind of life we've had, an exciting
testimony of salvation from wickedness or a long life
simply lived for God, He treasures our praise.

God didn't expect His angels to be saved from
deep sin before He'd accept their praise, and He doesn't
require it of us either. Though some go through hard
times before they come to the Lord and others sail
smoothly into His harbor, we all can glorify His name
because no matter how exciting our testimony is, the
glory always belongs to Him.

BE HAPPY

So be happy when you are insulted for being a Christian,
for then the glorious Spirit of God rests upon you.

1 PETER 4:14 NLT

God is telling us to be happy when others insult us for being Christians? What is that all about?

Peter was writing to first-century Christians who suffered for their faith. Persecution was part of the life of the church, and no doubt the people of that age didn't relish it any more than we do. So Peter turned their thoughts from the pain to the glory of God.

Insults are small potatoes when it comes to the kind of persecution that could land on us, but even harsh words bring the glory of His Spirit into our lives. So this holiday, let's not seek out persecution, but if someone criticizes our faith, we need not respond with anger. Instead let's think of God's glory and be thankful our testimony was clear enough to deserve it.

Word of the Father
WORD OF THE FATHER

God created everything through him, and
nothing was created except through him.

JOHN 1:3 NLT

"In the beginning the Word already existed. The Word was with God, and the Word was God," declares John 1:1 (NLT). "O Come, All Ye Faithful" is right; Jesus is the Word of the Father. No separation exists between them.

John 1:2–5 describes this Word. Though the ideas in the passage might seem a bit repetitive, they make sure we do not misunderstand the point God wants to make: Jesus wasn't created; He is God's Son, and as God, He created absolutely everything. No loopholes here. This passage repeats the ideas over and over so no one can argue against these truths.

Have we understood that the baby, the boy, the man He became were God enfleshed? Do we accept that He was God even before one star, one blade of grass, one animal was made? Then we have begun to know Jesus, Word of the Father.

FOUNTAIN OF LIFE

In him was life; and the life was the light of men.

JOHN 1:4 KJV

All our efforts to live life to the fullest pale compared to the energy that exudes from Jesus. And until we know Him, our lives are likewise thin and meaningless.

But when we accept Him as the One whom God sent for our salvation and put all our faith in Him, His light and life blaze into our lives. In a moment we feel as if we'd never lived before and understand that *this* is what God meant life to be, and because of it, we live differently.

Without Jesus, the Word, the fountain of life won't spring up in us, but once it flows within, it never stops. Sometimes it may run nearly silently; other times it's so powerful it roars in our ears. But the fountain of life never leaves us as long as we trust in Him.

Let's live in the Light.

LIVING CHRISTMAS

Anyone who says, "I know Him," but does not
obey His teaching is a liar. . . . But whoever obeys
His Word has the love of God made perfect in
him. . . . The one who says he belongs to Christ
should live the same kind of life Christ lived.

1 JOHN 2:4–6 NLV

After coming to Jesus, we begin to know Him deeply through reading scripture, attending church, and fellowshipping with other believers. For those who celebrate their first Christmas in the faith, this one will be special as they rejoice in that new experience.

But God doesn't simply call people to know about Him. Reading the Word is good, but living it out is even better. When we physically experience what God describes in the Bible, we draw even closer to the One who gave it to us. Sharing Christ's lifestyle brings understanding that reading words, even such inspired ones, cannot bring.

Celebrate the Savior, walk with Him in generosity of spirit and giving, and you will be living Christmas, too.

HIS TRUTH

For the word of the LORD is right, and all His work
is done in truth. He loves righteousness and justice;
the earth is full of the goodness of the LORD.

PSALM 33:4–5 NKJV

What would it be like to have perfectly consistent lives in which we never said one thing and did another? How would we feel if all our actions were good and right?

That's what it's like to be God. Nothing changes for Him. He never puts one thing in His written Word and leads us in another direction through His still, small voice. Jesus didn't say one thing and the prophets another. God's word, in whatever form it takes, continually reflects His nature, and His righteousness, justice, and goodness never change.

If it's God's truth, it shines with those unchanging qualities. If they're missing, we know our Lord is missing, too.

TINY BABE,
POWERFUL LORD

*The Son radiates God's own glory and expresses the
very character of God, and he sustains everything
by the mighty power of his command. When he had
cleansed us from our sins, he sat down in the place of
honor at the right hand of the majestic God in heaven.*

HEBREWS 1:3 NLT

The baby who lay in a manger became the Savior
who went to the cross. Based on that humble life,
few people would have imagined He'd become the Lord
described in this verse.

So often in our world, humble beginnings lead to
humble endings. Babies born in mangers live in humble
cottages and die a normal death, and we can't see beyond
it. But Jesus was no ordinary person. Everything about
Him radiated God, and though the world didn't much
like that, it didn't change the truth of His glory.

Can we see beyond our Lord's humble beginnings?
Will we believe that the humble Savior really rules in
heaven and on earth?

PICTURE OF GOD

No one has ever seen God. But the unique
One, who is himself God, is near to the
Father's heart. He has revealed God to us.

JOHN 1:18 NLT

Do we pride ourselves on being close to God? Knowing Him deeply and seeking to obey Him? Whatever we've done to draw close to our Lord is nothing compared to the intimacy between Father and Son. Jesus knows the Father's thoughts and plans. He Himself is God, intertwined with the Father in a way we cannot understand.

But Jesus doesn't hoard that knowledge; He brings it to us. Though we cannot know everything about the Father, He gives us a brief, accurate description of the One who loved us enough to send Him to us. Through Him we know what God asks of us and how He has come to us.

Need to see God? Just look at Jesus.

FULL STORY

The Word became flesh and made his dwelling among us. We have seen his glory, the glory of the one and only Son, who came from the Father, full of grace and truth.

JOHN 1:14 NIV

This is the miracle of Christmas—God come to earth. Had the story ended there, the wonderful event might touch our hearts, but would it have changed us from the inside out, made us new people?

Had God only given us the nice story of the baby, we'd never have experienced His sacrifice or been made right with God through His blood (Hebrews 9:22). We'd never have known how much grace and truth the Father could show to those who'd rejected Him.

But Jesus' Good Friday sacrifice and resurrection made us wholly right with God and allowed us to see His glory. The full story of redemption only starts with a baby in a manger—it ends in the glory of the One who suffered on the cross.

Do you know that both Jesus' birth and His sacrifice were all for you?

SECURITY

*"The grass withers and the flowers fall,
but the word of our God endures forever."*

Isaiah 40:8 niv

Our words last about as long as they take to leave our lips. The encouragement or hurt they cause may last longer. Still, we'd at least hope the hurtful ones would never last forever.

God's word is different. When He says something, those words are absolute truth—they will never change, not one single iota. He won't decide that this word needs some editing or that idea has gone out of style. What God says, He means.

When that Word is His Son, Jesus, how much less there's any likelihood that it would be changeable or less than reliable. The perfect One He sent to earth has no flaw in word or deed. Otherwise, He never could have died for our sins.

Grass, flowers, and our words are fleeting, but not the words of our Lord. We know what to expect of His Word every day. *That's* security.

PRACTICE MAKES PERFECT

Jesus replied, "But even more blessed are all who hear the word of God and put it into practice."

Going to church and hearing a good sermon can feel very satisfying. We love to hear a good, Word-based talk that helps us understand our Lord. But the Word isn't just for listening to. Jesus understood that when He drove this point home after preaching to a doubting crowd.

We can spend all day reading the Word and listen constantly to sermons, but unless we put the Word where it belongs, it's unproductive. If we read about love and never offer it to others, we are mere clanging cymbals (1 Corinthians 13:1); we can prattle about faith, but if we don't stand firm in difficult times, we hardly know what it means.

Only when we make Bible truths part of our lives are we living as if they mattered. When we practice what we hear, our faith is made perfect in the One who calls us to practice.

BELIEVE IT?

At that time the Roman emperor, Augustus,
decreed that a census should be taken throughout
the Roman Empire. (This was the first census
taken when Quirinius was governor of Syria.)

LUKE 2:1–2 NLT

*I*t would seem that this is a wonderful verse that makes the timing of Jesus' birth perfectly clear. After all, doesn't it tell us who was ruling in Rome and Syria?

It would be nice if things were that simple. Scholars say Quirinius was legate of Syria from AD 6 to 9. But Matthew 2:19–20 tells us that Joseph brought Jesus and Mary back to Nazareth after Herod died, in 4 BC. So this is a scripture that may require real faith.

Either we accept the validity of scripture or we don't. We believe, accepting that God's Word is true, or we throw out scripture, bankrupting our belief on the word of people. In time, new scholarship may discover the truth of scripture, but how would that help if we'd trusted in today's fallible scholars for our eternal destiny?

KNOWING THE WORD

Soon the news reached the apostles and other believers in Judea that the Gentiles had received the word of God.

ACTS 11:1 NLT

When Jesus walked the earth, the apostles and other Christians saw Him. They could testify to the words He spoke and the message His actions conveyed, because they had seen the Word and learned from Him.

But what of those of us who have never seen the Word of God, Jesus, in the flesh? We are like the Gentiles in this verse, who had never seen Jesus walk the earth. Yet they, too, knew the Word, through His message, sent by way of the apostles who came to spread the Good News.

Though we've never walked with the Word enfleshed, His words come to us as clearly as they did to those first-century Gentiles, through the scriptures and the Spirit. No matter what distance of time and space lies between us, we can know Him as surely as if He walked concrete sidewalks with us.

NEARNESS

Come near to God and he will come near to you.

JAMES 4:8 NIV

God's Word promises He will always be near us (Hebrews 13:5). So what's happening when, right in the middle of December, we start feeling bored with Christmas and God? We've gone to the Advent services and sung the carols with vigor, but something is missing. We just don't feel the joy.

Maybe, for all the wonderful services and opportunities to fellowship, we've been less than faithful in other ways. If holiday events have pushed our private devotions out of our schedules, we may need to recommit to them. If our prayers have been halfhearted, perhaps we need to reconsider the needs of others. Or unconfessed sin may be the barrier that keeps us from Him.

He will not desert us, but we may cause the distance. If we'll take that first step in faith, we'll find He's just one step away.

GOD'S TRUTH

*Therefore the Lord himself shall give you a
sign; Behold, a virgin shall conceive, and bear
a son, and shall call his name Immanuel.*

Isaiah 7:14 KJV

Doubters love to debate this verse and claim that the Hebrew word used for "virgin" simply means a young woman of an age to marry. Though the word can be used that way, often it means just what we usually associate with that word. And the Jews who translated the Old Testament into Greek (the Septuagint) reflected their understanding when they used a Greek word that also means a young woman who has never known a man sexually.

We can't take cues from the doubters who have no idea what God had in mind, or we will find ourselves with bankrupt faith. What knowledge of Hebrew do they have? What intimacy with God can inform their claims?

Instead, we can trust both Old and New Testament documents, God's Word and truth for all.

WORK IN PROGRESS

"Anyone who loves me will obey my teaching.
My Father will love them, and we will come
to them and make our home with them."

JOHN 14:23 NIV

Have you ever had trouble obeying the scriptures? Surely you knew just what they required of you, but hard as you tried, complete obedience eluded you.

You're not alone. God's call to obey His Word is challenging because it heads Christians in another direction—one our sinful hearts aren't comfortable with. It can take a long time to learn to do what Jesus commands. And some things we may never get quite right.

But good news! God hasn't left us alone in our struggle. When we accept Jesus, God comes to live with us. Where we go, He goes, too. And His Spirit works in our lives, empowering us to increasingly obey His Word.

We may not be perfect, but we are a successful work in progress. Loved by the Father, we find our lives increasingly turning to obedience and love. And His works never fail.

TAKE THE WORD

I saw heaven standing open and there before
me was a white horse, whose rider is called
Faithful and True. With justice he judges and
wages war. . . . He is dressed in a robe dipped
in blood, and his name is the Word of God.

REVELATION 19:11, 13 NIV

Today everyone on earth can take the Word or leave Him. Some live in the light of His truth, while others ignore or deny it. Believers and nonbelievers grow together like wheat and weeds.

But one day, the One whose truth has been ignored will weed things out. With His heavenly army, Jesus will "strike down the nations." Then He will be recognized as the "King of kings and Lord of lords" (Revelation 19:15–16 NIV).

No longer a simple baby or a carpenter in Galilee, the Word's glorious nature will shine forth, to the distress of those who have denied Him.

So if you want to be on the winning side, take the Word—don't leave Him.

SCRIPTURE INDEX